WILLIAM SHAKESPEARE

First published in Great Britain in 1999 by Brockhampton Press
a member of the Hodder Headline Group
20 Bloomsbury Street, London WC1B 3QA

ISBN 1-86019-9763

A copy of the CIP data is available from the
British Library upon request.

Designed and produced for Brockhampton Press
by Keith Pointing Design Consultancy.

Reprographics by Global Colour
Printed in Singapore.

Image of Henry Wriothesley, 3rd Earl of Southampton, by unknown artist,
by courtesy of the National portrait Gallery, London

WILLIAM SHAKESPEARE

A BIOGRAPHY WITH
THE COMPLETE SONNETS

ANDREW LAMBIRTH

BROCKHAMPTON PRESS
LONDON

CONTENTS

WILLIAM SHAKESPEARE

Introduction

It MAY sound strange, but biographers and literary historians have long fantasized about finding one of William Shakespeare's laundry lists. It has become a commonplace of Shakespeare studies - one of those few facts known even to the general reader - that so little is known about the man who wrote so wisely, that an inventory of his undergarments would actually shed new light on his personality. So it might. It would also excite endless speculation, without adding a great deal to our store of facts.

All Shakespeare enthusiasts face the same dilemma: the difficulty of separating fact from fiction. But it should not be forgotten that the Shakespeare myth has a value of its own. The stories which have accumulated around this shadowy figure - there are several very different portraits of him, but the one most often accepted to be true depicts a man prematurely bald with fiddle-shaped brows - have in fact helped to popularize him. Shakespeare is human and fallible, whether as poacher or poet, as lover or dramatist, as absentee father or would-be gentleman. The facts flesh out the myth, and only make it more enduring.

For instance, one aspect of the legend interprets him as a high-spirited frequenter of taverns and a charming seducer of the ladies. As a gloss on this, local Midlands gossip still maintains that Shakespeare had no head for drink and that he managed to get several doses of clap. He is not a dusty figure from ancient history; he has become a kind of living folk spirit, with magic in the invocation of his name.

We don't even know for sure when he was born. This supposed mystery - or at the very least, lack of evidence - about Shakespeare's life has led to a proliferation of alternative theories of authorship. Rival candidates abound, for how could an uncultured bumpkin like this man from Stratford have written with such beauty, knowledge and understanding? Obviously, a noble of the Court must have been responsible, or so the story runs. Over the centuries various pretenders have been advanced, from the great play-wright of *Tamburlaine* and *Doctor Faustus*, Christopher Marlowe, to Francis Bacon, essayist and inventor, first baron Verulam. According to different reports and theories, Shakespeare was either the Earl of Oxford, the Earl of Rutland or the Earl of Derby, or the Countess of Pembroke, or Walter Raleigh, or Queen Elizabeth I herself. Yet there is less hard evidence to support any of these contenders than there is in favour of Shakespeare himself. The most important thing we have to do is make a leap of faith - we have to grant Shakespeare the power of imagination. Is that really so hard?

Everything is there in the Sonnets, they are like an entire Renaissance world in microcosm. And like a complete life, there are areas of

POET'S WALK, ETON, BY THE THAMES

mystery and unclearness as well. We will probably never be able fully to define or categorize the Sonnets, and that it just as well. The scientific thirst to find an explanation for everything is dangerous. Some things should remain opaque. Shakespeare enlivens life by his joy, his profound despair, and his humour. Whether dealing in ruin or rapture, Shakespeare leaves a lasting impression of language finely honed to a pitch of perfect expression.

One sure measure of a writer's fame lies in the degree to which his words have entered everyday parlance. The language of love poetry would not be what it is today without Shakespeare, and several of the Sonnets have entered the mainstream. Particular lines like 'Shall I compare thee to a summer's day?' are formidable in their popularity. Not that everyone who quotes them actually knows who wrote them, but in some ways that is even more remarkable, for it means that there is no way of bettering what they say, and that they have been unequivocally accepted.

A line such as 'brave day sunk in hideous night' (Sonnet 12), or 'remembrance of things past' (Sonnet 30), or 'time's thievish progress to eternity' (Sonnet 77), or 'when in the chronicle of wasted time' (Sonnet 106), stirs echoes through our island's literary and oral traditions. And these are only examples taken from the Sonnets, there are many more quotes from the plays that have assumed an everyday truth and relevance. Shakespeare was the consummate theatre-poet whose genius touches us today as readily as it ever did.

THE AVON AT STRATFORD

FARMHOUSE IN HYDE LANE NEAR MARBLE ARCH

Early Life

The surprising truth is that we actually do know quite a lot about Shakespeare's life. When you pause to consider that he was a provincial, and that records were still really in their infancy, we have to admit we know him really quite well. William Shakespeare came from the Midlands of Britain, hard by the beautiful Cotswolds. There had been Shakespeares in Warwickshire since at least the mid 13th century, a respected name though spelt with a certain variety and freedom. Alternatively Shogspar, Choxper, Shagspere, Shake-scene and Shaxpere, the different spellings matched the exceptional fluidity of the period. The Elizabethan Age was one of tremendous creativity, of new ideas and discoveries, of almost constant change and development. Among the buccaneers like Sir Francis Drake and the financiers such as Sir Thomas Gresham moved the writers and poets, and premier among these was Shakespeare.

In April 1564, quite possibly on the twenty-third, which is St George's Day, William, the eldest of four boys and two girls, was born in Stratford-upon-Avon to John Shakespeare, a glover by trade, an ambitious business man and a fairly prominent local politician, and Mary Arden, youngest daughter of a local great landowning family. William was actually the third child of the Shakespeares, but the first to survive infancy. It seems that his mother was sufficiently well-educated to write, and that she taught the boy to do so too. It's quite probable that Shakespeare was close to his mother, and that his knowledge of her enabled him to understand how women think and feel, which is one of the hallmarks of his writing. Shakespeare, an impressively courteous boy, grew up managing to avoid the plague, which carried off one in every fifteen in the parish. His father became mayor or High Bailiff of Stratford, a borough town of some size and importance, during the late 1560s. But he pushed his luck too far, dealt illegally in the wool trade, and lost both money and property.

Aged thirteen, Shakespeare went to grammar school, along with the rest of the town's elite, as a son of commerce united with aristocracy. Here he would have had to memorize Latin, which would have helped to train his ear. He would also have discovered Ovid's *Metamorphoses*, one of his favourite books, and a great source of stories he could later adapt.

It seems that in 1581-2 he spent some months in a different part of the country, and it may have been the case that he worked for a while as a private tutor in Lancashire. Various legends have grown up around the young Shakespeare - that he was caught poaching deer (a late tradition this) on the neighbouring great estate of Charlecote, or that he became a teacher, or a lawyer's clerk, or for some reason travelled abroad at an early age. Most theories smack too much of the picturesque, but recent research suggests that he may well have been employed briefly to give private tuition in the

THE GRAMMAR SCHOOL, STRATFORD-ON-AVON

ANN HATHAWAY'S COTTAGE

north of England.

In 1582, aged eighteen and thus still technically a minor, he married Anne Hathaway, who was eight years his senior. At twenty-five or twenty-six Anne might seem old and on the shelf, but it was in fact quite usual for the professional classes to marry at this age. It seems that the Hathaways had long known the Shakespeares. But was it a shotgun wedding? The first child was certainly quick enough in arriving. In 1583 the couple had a daughter named Susanna, and two years later twins christened Hamnet and Judith. Shakespeare was not necessarily trapped into marriage. He may well have chosen it deliberately, relishing the security if offered since it provided him with the kind of support he needed from which to launch himself. This is a typical strategy among creative people, who reserve all their invention and imagination for their work, while remaining outwardly conventional. (Look at Flaubert, for example.)

Rural Warwicksire is the background and sounding board of all Shakespeare's writings. He knew the countryside intimately and used it as a refreshing source of imagery, however urban some of his stories may have been. Stratford's link with London (there is some hundred miles between them) was Clopton Bridge over the River Avon, built by Sir Hugh Clopton (died 1492), a former Lord Mayor of London, who also built the domestic dwelling New Place which Shakespeare was himself to purchase once he could afford it.

QUEEN ELIZABETH

What was the complexion of Elizabethan society? Queen Elizabeth I had united the kingdom under Protestantism, though there still remained an external Catholic threat in the form of Spain, and an internal one in the shape of Mary Queen of Scots. England still had a sizeable Catholic population, but it was kept under close scrutiny and frequently fined. In 1587 Mary Queen of Scots was tried and executed, and the Catholic threat was instantly diminished, especially when the Spanish Armada was so successfully quashed the following year. Under Elizabeth, England became a great maritime power.

In cultural terms, what was happening? There was, for instance, no tradition of secular drama to replace the old religious Mystery Plays, but a brand-new style was already developing. Nicholas Udall, headmaster of Eton, had written the first English comedy, entitled *Ralph Roister Doister* (c1552), and Sackville and Norton the first tragedy, called *Gorboduc* (1561). Queen Elizabeth, herself a rare intellectual (the only one ever to occupy the English throne) and a great lover of plays, encouraged the development of the drama.

Whatever he may have been doing beforehand, it appears that by 1587 Shakespeare was in London, possibly through the intervention of his Stratford friend Dick Field, who had come to the capital as an apprentice printer. London was rich and colourful, filled with shops and houses, painted theatres and palaces. It was gorgeous, but filthy. London Bridge had houses and shops upon it, three storeys high. Many people were literate, but it was still a violent city. The large body of apprentices frequently rioted and thought nothing of breaking heads. Brawls and cut-purse gangs abounded. Sex was everywhere: girls even solicited inside St Paul's Cathedral.

Somehow Shakespeare had to make a living, so he joined a company of actors, a profession not unknown to the son of Stratford's former Chamberlain (1562-6), one of whose tasks was to pay the strolling actors who came to entertain the Stratfordians. (In particular the Queen's Players and the Earl of Worcester's Men.) And although Shakespeare no doubt yearned to be a poet, he was put to the re-working of blank verse plays. (These are written in verse without rhyme, particularly in the iambic pentameter, a metrical form of great flexibility.) There was a growing appetite for the theatre as escapism, as a temporary release from drudgery. The earliest known free-standing theatre dates from 1567, situated out Whitechapel way. By the 1590s, the main playhouses were the Theatre and the Curtain, both in Shoreditch, and the Rose in Southwark.

Intellectually, Shakespeare stole from wherever he could: he a dapted stories from ballads, he overheard anecdotes at court when performing in the royal presence, he scoured the history books and the classics. Something of a chameleon, he borrowed and assimilated widely. His mind was agile and he was observant and quick-witted. In those days writers of plays were called poets, not yet playwrights. They were paid little, and

CHURCH IN SPRINGTIME

were scarcely much further up the social ladder than actors who were frequently attacked in print and pulpit as ungodly, obscene and sexually dubious. (Boys took the female roles - in bed, no doubt, as often as they had to on the boards.)

A demanding repertory system was in force, with a different play being acted every day of the week. Shakespeare, beginning as a hireling actor, would have had to take 100 small parts in a season, and each acting company needed 15 or 20 new plays a year. This put tremendous strain on the writers who, for the most part, were gentlemen with Oxford or Cambridge degrees, like the so-called University Wits and pamphleteers - Thomas Nashe, Robert Green and George Peele. In this company Shakespeare stood out as a mere grammar-school man, and an actor to boot! Only a few names survive because the dramatists - as have Hollywood scriptwriters more recently - have remained largely anonymous.

Robert Greene for one was to cause Shakespeare trouble, albeit posthumously. Greene resented the younger man, his social inferior and rival, who had the temerity to steal his ideas. (Shakespeare had no hesitation in borrowing a good plot wherever he found one.) Greene died in near-poverty and in 1592 his last publication appeared, entitled *Greenes Groats-worth of Witte,* in which he referred to Shakespeare as 'an upstart Crow, beautified with our feathers'. Did such calumny damage Shakespeare's reputation? Probably not, though it may have hurt his pride. He was already supported by influential men of rank, particularly among the Inns of Court, of which Gray's Inn was the largest and most fashionable. Traditionally the Inns sponsored the drama, for they were filled by young students from wealthy families with time on their hands, many of them also given to the reading and writing of sonnets.

In the summer of 1592, the plague grew so intense that by government order the theatres of London (as dens of infection) were closed. They were to remain closed until the summer of 1594. What did Shakespeare do in this interval? The other players would have gone off on tour around the country to avoid the plague and earn a crust at one and the same time. It seems that Shakespeare did not accompany them. He had established a certain name and reputation by 1592. At this point he took to writing poetry, quite possibly returning to Stratford to do so. It seems likely that the Sonnets were mostly written during this period, though their precise dating remains in doubt.

What is a Sonnet?

A sonnet is a poem of 14 lines, with 10 syllables per line in English (11 in Italian, 12 in French) with a particular rhyme scheme. Petrarch (1304-74) pioneered the sonnet form and was much imitated by 16th century writers such as Sir Philip Sidney (1554-86), whose *Astrophel and Stella* sonnet sequence proved very popular. Sidney would have been an influence on Shakespeare, as would Marlowe, but Shakespeare brought something very much of his own to the form. The rhyme scheme that he favoured is notated as follows: a b a b c d c d e f e f g g. (The other famous schemes are the Petrarchian variant, which begins a b b a a b b a, and the Miltonic.) The subject of the sonnet was usually love.

Shakespeare abandoned Petrarch's rhythmic form and built up a contemporary version of it, with three quatrains and a final couplet. This was done in search of sweetness, for the music of the words. The first eight lines, or octave, were to set up an argument, often contradicted by the following six lines, or sestet. For today's ear, nurtured on free verse and pop lyrics, the sonnet will perhaps seem overly contrived and too forcibly structured. Its chief features are compression and immediacy. The cumulative effect of the piling up of words is both intense and economic, and requires consummate linguistic discipline to work at all well.

As Wordsworth wrote in a sonnet of his own: 'Scorn not the sonnet...with this key/Shakespeare unlocked his heart...' The story of Shakespeare's Sonnets is a mythical one. They are mainly addressed to a beautiful young man who steals the poet's mistress (the Dark Lady) and then seems to transfer his favour to another poet. To what extent is this based in fact? To what extent indeed is it intended to be thought of as a real story, rather than as a useful fictional formula, accepted as nothing but a framework upon which to display the brilliance of Master Shakespeare's wordplay? In the end we don't know, and the whole situation has been confused and complicated by the ambiguous dedication of the Sonnets. The first part of this reads as follows:

To the Only Begetter of

These Insuing Sonnets

Mr WH All Happiness

And that Eternity

Promised

By

Our Everliving Poet

The controversy centres on the identity of Mr WH. The principal suspects are Henry Wriothesley, 3rd Earl of Southampton (his initials inverted), William Herbert, the future Earl of Pembroke, who was only 12 in 1592 when many of the Sonnets are thought to have been written, and Henry

HENRY WRIOTHESLEY, 3RD EARL OF SOUTHAMPTON

Willoughby (initials again inverted), a minor poet of unrequited love. Of course, it may be none of them. Perhaps Thomas Thorpe, the publisher of the Sonnets, simply invented a mysterious dedication to act as a kind of sales pitch or lure.

Of the principal suspects, Southampton seems the likeliest, partly because Shakespeare had already dedicated both his long poems to him. In April 1593, Shakespeare published his long erotic poem, *Venus and Adonis*, with a fulsome inscription to Southampton. Did he really aspire to his lordship's friendship? The class system would have conspired against any such familiarity, but there have always been private patrons whose personal idiosyncracies or interests made them flout the rules. *Venus and Adonis* was sexy and popular, and helped to make Shakespeare much better known. By 1599 it had gone through at least half-a-dozen editions, and was much talked about. In 1594 Shakespeare consolidated this success by publishing *The Rape of Lucrece,* another long poem in a similar vein, and also dedicated to Southampton.

Who was this noble? In 1593, Southampton was nineteen and very handsome; he was also wealthy. He was a member of Gray's Inn, which operated both as a law school and a sort of finishing school of manners. He was cultivated and well-connected. It's quite likely that Shakespeare became one of his retinue. But were they lovers? Anthony Burgess concludes that this wasn't necessarily the case. He suggests that Shakespeare merely

THE THAMES FROM WINDSOR

wanted to convey an aesthetic shock by writing about friendship in the language of heterosexual love. This is perfectly likely. The sonnet tradition was not fixated on truth. Quite often poets wrote sonnets for the sheer pleasure of inventing exquisite verses, which they then addressed to an imaginary mistress.

In 1598, Francis Meres, an aspiring literary critic, referred to Shakespeare as 'mellifluous and honey-tongued' and claimed that what he called the 'sugared' Sonnets were circulated among Shakespeare's friends. ('Sugared' here means smooth and graceful.) Manuscripts were no doubt copied out and passed from hand to hand, but Shakespeare would have had very little control over this. Indeed the first edition of the Sonnets was not published until 1609, and even then perhaps without Shakespeare's permission, for no law of copyright as yet existed.

Certainly it seems that Shakespeare enjoyed a high reputation among the wits and blades of the Inns of Court, and in some circles he was known as 'William the Conqueror'. This nickname may derive from a slightly scurrilous tale which was then doing the rounds. It was said that after a performance of Richard III, the actor taking the role of Richard (Dick Burbage) had arranged to meet up with a female admirer. Shakespeare overheard the assignation and contrived to arrive at the lady's room before Burbage, and even to take his place. When expectant Burbage was announced, Shakespeare simply sent this message via the servant: that William the Conqueror had come before Richard III...

There is a major problem of dating the Sonnets. It's possible that they were written over a considerable period of time, from the 1580s into the new century, which would account for the fact that they are by no means equal in quality or interest. Some are merely literary exercises; perhaps they were addressed to a specifically *literary* patron, a patron of letters (but who? Southampton still?). Others are conventional exercises in the writing of love poetry to a boy and then to a girl.

The Sonnets are largely about how time destroys us so quickly. They might easily have been written when the poet was young and worried by the prospect of ageing. They alternate wildly abstract assertions with concrete images drawn directly from experience of life. They cover a range of emotions from joy to bitterness and disillusion.

It was part of the sonnet-writer's job to be mysterious and cleverly convoluted. Sonnets were often written in code to afford the recipient delight in their de-coding. Today we are impatient in taking our pleasures and want instant transparency of meaning. That was the reverse of fashionable in Shakespeare's day. Sonnets were conventionally melancholy in tone, but the Renaissance concept of man's self had not before appeared with such prominence as subject matter. Shakespeare's soul was troubled and he poured out his anxiety and restlessness into these poetic vessels.

The sonnet form, gathered here into a collection or sequence of individual poems, as opposed to one long poem of 154 x 14 lines (or 2156 lines), allows Shakespeare greater technical freedom. A long poem can be unwieldy. The sonnet is like a swift English ship, deft and deadly. It allows him to dart about but also to hark back, to repeat, to polish and perfect. Also to reproach. That was very useful. He had a lot apparently to complain about. Not all the 154 are perfect or conventional sonnets. Sonnet 99, for instance, is the only one to run to fifteen lines. Sonnet 126 consists of six rhymed iambic couplets. The Elizabethans used the term 'sonnet' quite loosely, meaning simply a short lyrical poem, following the original Italian *sonnetto*, meaning a little song.

The Sonnets were Shakespeare's great bid to win respectability as a poet, rather than as an actor or theatre writer. His greatest ambition was to be a gentleman with a coat of arms, and he thought to achieve this through writing. In those days, prose was for recipes and history, it was not art; but poetry was. Shakespeare hoped to gain honour through poetry, which in a sense he did. But it was not to make his fortune. Perhaps he realized that the sonnet form was already going out of fashion. Perhaps he came to the end of himself as a pure poet. Whatever the reason, he turned full-time to the making of plays. Never again did he write long poems, nor invent more sonnets, though there are songs aplenty and all manner of dramatic poetry in the plays.

THE MEANING OF THE SONNETS

Shakespeare's Sonnets have a general overriding theme of almost idolatrous love for a youth, but don't look for one continuous story in these short self-contained poems. We can't even be certain that they were written in the order in which they were published. Nor do we know for sure whether Shakespeare merely projected himself imaginatively into states of mind he himself never experienced, as the good fiction writer must be able to do, or if the Sonnets are truly confessional. It seems likely that they are a mixture of the two, but quite what the proportions are we'll probably never know.

The Sonnets demonstrate a huge relish for paradox. Their main theme is love, which has always resisted easy explanation. So Shakespeare resorts to contradiction and ambiguity. He is inward-turning, reflective, even inward-dwelling. It's as if he is trying to reach a definition of self: Man as the centre of the universe; Man increasingly preoccupied with self-definition. At their worst, the Sonnets are portentous-sounding, though they are never dull. From the internal evidence of the Sonnets it appears that Shakespeare experienced emotions intensely. Or perhaps just that he was young when he wrote them. Despite the ambiguities, the Sonnets encompass a profound exploration of love, with something almost ruthless (certainly not self-sparing) shaping the investigation.

Graham Greene called 'Desiring this man's art, and that man's scope', from Sonnet 29, 'perhaps the most startling line of poetry in all our literature'. But this is to be too literal. Greene asks how could such a magnificent artist as Shakespeare have envied anyone? This begs two questions: one that he meant it in a straightforward sense, and two that Shakespeare had no grain of humility or self-doubt in him. Whichever, Greene's seems too autobiographical an approach. The great artist transcends mere autobiography (or makes it everything - and Shakespeare certainly didn't do that), transmuting daily experience into timeless observation.

It seems that the Sonnets were written expressly for private view, and it's unlikely that many people actually read them, though no doubt plenty would have talked as if they had. Perhaps Shakespeare prevented their publication, knowing them to reveal too much of his innermost thoughts and feelings. They certainly weren't published in his mother's lifetime, which may be significant. (Professor Park Honan thinks it is. Mary Shakespeare died in September 1608, and the first edition of the Sonnets was not until the following year.) There again, there are more manuscript copies of Sonnet 2 surviving from the 17th century than of any other. What does this tell us? Merely that the taste of one age rarely survives into another.

It wasn't until the 18th century that the belief became widespread that the characters in the Sonnets corresponded to real people in Shakespeare's own life. There's no reason to think they have to, but our own late 20th century passion for deciphering the life in the work makes this a popular pursuit today. So who was the Dark Lady? One theory suggests that she was John Florio's wife. (He was tutor and then secretary to the Earl of Southampton and the translator of Montaigne.) Another that she was a whore in the stews of Clerkenwell. She may have been dark complexioned, or just dark-haired, or perhaps of mixed blood - a mulatto or an octaroon. Who knows? Anthony Burgess makes the convincing suggestion that she was a composite creature, the fruit of more than one experience.

The first 17 sonnets are addressed to a young man with whom the writer appears to be in love, but whom he also entreats to get married and beget children. It's easy to imagine a fond but concerned parent commissioning Shakespeare to write these sonnets in order to put pressure on their hesitant son. Why else should he have harped on the same subject so insistently? At this period it was permissable for a man to have very intimate friendships with other men, although actual buggery was against the law. The Sonnets are undoubtedly homoerotic, and begin to suggest that women are essentially for child-bearing, whereas real companionship is reserved for males. This idea was however to be revised in the Dark Lady Sonnets.

In Sonnet 1, the sweet declaration 'contracted to thine own bright eyes' chimes well with the exact observation of spring being 'gaudy'. The remarkable thing is how various these single-themed sonnets can be. Shakespeare addresses sentiment without being sentimental: 'Thou art thy mother's glass, and she in thee/Calls back the lovely April of her prime' (Sonnet 3). In Sonnet 5 the imagery of time's lapsing adopts the figure of extracting perfume: 'summer's distillation left/A liquid pris'ner pent in walls of glass'. In this sonnet and the following one there is much use of the concept of distilling, and distillation is indeed what Shakespeare achieves in his own writing. (It's a subject to which he returns in Sonnet 54.) He can be literal or oblique. In Sonnet 6 the line 'make sweet some vial' means to impregnate a woman's womb. In Sonnet 9, 'Is it for fear to wet a widow's eye/That thou consum'st thyself in single life?' is a clever and pretty conceit.

As with all great poetry, images remain in the mind, and though their meaning is repetitious they do not bore because of their skilful invention. Look at another of these procreative exhortations, Sonnet 11: 'She [meaning Nature] carved thee for her seal, and meant thereby/Thou shouldst print more, not let that copy die.' Very effective. Shakespeare relished multiple meanings. For instance, in Sonnet 16, which is altogether the best of the propagation poems, 'lines of life' towards the end of the sonnet can refer equally to the young man's figure (his outline), the wrinkles which one day may appear on his face, his descendants (his blood-line), lines drawn with a pencil in the making of a portrait, lines written with a pen, the lines of a poem (this Sonnet, for instance), and destiny (his life-line). What extraordinary compression!

At the same time Shakespeare is self-deprecating, referring to 'my barren rhyme'. This stands in direct contrast to the final couplet of Sonnet 18, which has good grounds to be considered the most famous of them all, particularly the first four lines. ('Shall I compare thee to a summer's day?'etc.) The final couplet reads 'So long as men can breathe or eyes can see,/So long lives this, and this gives life to thee.' It's a clear boast (and a justified one) that Shakespeare has the power to confer immortality on his beloved. Not that we know who he is, this golden boy. That's the poignant irony of it.

Sonnet 20 excites all those who want to believe that Shakespeare was bisexual. He refers elegantly here to 'the master mistress of my passion', but ends up suggesting that the beautiful boy (with the face of a girl) has been 'pricked out' by Nature 'for women's pleasure'. Which would seem to deny the poet's part. But then can you ever be certain when Shakespeare is being serious? In Sonnet 21 he throws in 'rondure', a pretty obscure word even by his generous standards. Some commentators believe he did it deliberately in order to mock his own poetic affectation.

In Sonnet 26, addressed to the 'Lord of my love...', there is some

SHEEP GRAZING BY RIVER

suggestion of showing his all (line 8: 'all naked'), which perhaps is a coded sexual reference. We cannot be sure. Shakespeare deals in puns and wordplay, but rarely explains what he intended. It's possible to put almost any construction, however far-fetched, on his words and have to admit he may have meant it. Sonnets 27 and 28 continue the same theme, and this emphasis suggests the importance of a hidden message. There's still plenty of room for speculation. Sexual innuendo is rife within these poems.

There are also echoes of proverbs in many of the sonnets. It's as if Shakespeare alludes to that fund of popular wisdom to reinforce his arguments and to make them more memorable. Perhaps it was a habit he picked up from listening to too many Sunday sermons in his youth. The last line of Sonnet 33 'Suns of the world may stain when heav'n's sun staineth' seems to carry an echo of Chaucer's familiar 'If gold rust what shall iron do?' And in Sonnet 95 there is what has been described as a phallic proverb: 'The hardest knife ill used doth lose his edge'. Sonnet 102 would appear to make reference in the line 'sweets grown common lose their dear delight' to the proverb 'Familiarity breeds contempt'.

The first five lines of Sonnet 35 are very good: the images flash simply and clearly - 'Roses have thorns, and silver fountains mud,/Clouds and eclipses stain both moon and sun,' and Shakespeare makes the philosophical point that he himself is not without fault. In the following poem, Sonnet 36, he alludes to the traditional metaphor by which lover and beloved are one. (And thus perhaps makes reference to the Platonic divided self, searching worldwide for its other half.) Was there any didactic purpose behind the Sonnets? Was Shakespeare trying to teach his golden boy, covering the lessons with deliberate posing and brilliant wit?

Certainly Shakespeare runs the whole gamut of emotions. Jealousy stalks through Sonnet 42, over the loss of a mistress and the loss of a friend. Again in Sonnet 61: 'me far off, with others all too near'. But in Sonnet 59 he is oddly embarrassed, almost ashamed of himself: 'O sure I am the wits of former days/To subjects worse have giv'n admiring praise.' Or is this just sarcasm? In Sonnet 62 he is disparaging of his own appearance 'Beated and chopped with tanned antiquity'. In Sonnet 66 Shakespeare is suddenly a list-maker of social abuses. He is deftly ambiguous as to who deserves to benefit and who does not. His images are self-cancelling. He speaks of 'captive good attending captain ill', of 'maiden virtue rudely strumpeted', of 'art made tongue-tied by authority.' Even when he's at his most seemingly abstruse, the writing of these poems must have been a great relief to his feelings. Besides offering proof of his immense verbal dexterity, as they were private productions he could say freely just what he liked.

Shakespeare evoked nature brilliantly, and used it to underline and shape his meaning. Sonnet 62 begins with a first line which is powerful and yet simple. 'Like as the waves make towards the pebbled shore...' Take out a single word, even the 'as', and the music is gone. Again, when in Sonnet 64 and writing of 'the hungry ocean', Shakespeare coins the line 'Increasing store with loss, and loss with store', it acts audibly as an echo of the tide's movement. One of the most beautiful lines of all comes in Sonnet 73 - 'Bare ruined choirs, where late the sweet birds sang'. Here Shakespeare invokes both an architectural simile and a vocal one. The leafless autumn trees arch upwards like the stone Choirs of the great cathedrals (those parts of large churches between the altar and the nave), while a choir is also a company of singers, whether birds or human beings. Again a rich image, saying much with considerable economy.

The verbal intelligence is exceptional in these poems. Sonnet 43 deals with mirror images, with shadows and objects, hinting that things are not what they seem to be, or not what they might be expected to be. The repetition of 'shadow' followed up by 'show', 'shade' and 'shine', underline the theme. Sonnet 45 continues the contradictions, the claimed duality (which always suggests sex), the 'present-absent'. The idea is extended through Sonnets 46 and 47 in a formulation very typical of the Renaissance, where the seen is contrasted with the felt, the eye with the heart, or in other words, mere infatuation with true love. It's an idea taken up again in Sonnets 24, 132 and 133, and 141.

Shakespeare was deeply aware of the pleasures of infrequency. In *Henry IV Part I* he has Prince Hal say 'If all the year were playing holidays, To sport would be as tedious as to work; But when they seldom come, they wish'd for come.' In Sonnet 52 he writes: 'Therefore are feasts so solemn and so rare,/Since seldom coming in the long year set,/Like stones of worth they thinly placed are,/Or captain jewels in the carcanet.' It's a truth of which we need constant reminding in this age of gross and indecent leisure and seasonal vegetables all year round. The same note is pursued in the couplet of Sonnet 56: 'As call it winter, which being full of care,/Makes summer's welcome, thrice more wished, more rare.'

Are we right to imagine Shakespeare rushing home in a heat and dashing off a sonnet? Given that the major themes deal so expertly with the human passions, it seems likely that they were fuelled by personal experience. And although some of the sonnets do seem to speak of emotion recollected in tranquillity, others may have had their original impetus from a quarrel or love pang and then been gradually refined over the following weeks. Shakespeare writes of real events (or imagines them brilliantly) but also deals with idealized love, that impossible state that all lovers seek and some think they've found.

Shakespeare talks of being his beloved's slave in Sonnet 57, and then prints him a licence to sin in the couplet: 'So true a fool is love, that in

MANOR HOUSE WITH DEER IN GARDEN

your will,/Though you do anything, he thinks no ill.' Play upon the word 'will' is inevitable: it's a shortened version of the poet's Christian name, it may also have been the name of his rival lover, it means desire, it denotes energy of intention, it stands for the male generative organ - and indeed at that time it meant vagina as well - it can be any or all of these at once. It appears twenty times in the pair of 'will' sonnets, 135 and 136. Can we imagine the recipient of the poems shrieking with laughter (as might a viewer of the subtler moments of a 'Carry On' film) when first reading them, or merely smiling? Is it not somewhat overdone? Perhaps there was extra hidden relevance.

Shakespeare has various ways of describing time apart from 'this bloody tyrant time' (Sonnet 16). A more subtle approach to time's ravages is sketched in Sonnet 15: 'When I consider everything that grows/Holds in perfection but a little moment...' The adjectives continue: 'devouring time' and 'swift-footed time' both feature in Sonnet 19. Shakespeare is obsessed with the passage of time. Did he fear his own extinction? He revolves between despair and the consolations of his art. Again in Sonnet 19: 'Yet do thy worst, old time; despite thy wrong,/My love shall in my verse ever live young.' In Sonnet 55 time is 'sluttish', but 'Not marble nor the gilded monuments/Of princes shall outlive this pow'rful rhyme...' Another first class example comes in Sonnet 60: 'Time doth transfix the flourish set on youth,/And delves the parallels in beauty's brow,/Feeds on the rarities of nature's truth...'

This near-constant harping on about time, age and death operates rather like a *vanitas* subject in painting or the *memento mori* (a death's head at the feast, the skull beneath the skin) so beloved of the age. It was intended to remind people that worldly things do not last, and that in life we are but a step, a moment away, from death. It's as if Shakespeare yearns towards dying - or pretends to for the sake of his poems. What will the beloved do if the lover should die? It's a stock argument which Shakespeare turns on its head with sweet sad resignation. The beloved will be fine, of course. And the world (the word?) and the spirit will continue.

When Shakespeare writes of 'Time's thievish progress' in Sonnet 77, he also mentions 'the vacant leaves' and 'these waste blanks'. Rather than some arcane sexual imagery, it has been suggested that this refers to a book of blank paper, perhaps intended as a commonplace book or journal, presented as a gift along with the sonnet. We might imagine Shakespeare encouraging the object of his adoration to begin himself to write and thus grasp after immortality.

How real is Shakespeare's modesty? Or was it assumed for the sake of writing the Sonnets? In Sonnet 78 he says categorically 'thou art all my art, and dost advance/As high as learning my rude ignorance.' But is anything ever categoric here? Sonnet 79 introduces the rival poet. Now was he real or invented? And if real, who might he have been - Marlowe, George

Chapman, Drayton? (Burgess is convinced it's Chapman.) In Sonnet 80 Shakespeare suddenly seems tongue in cheek: still dealing with rivalry, but in a different tone. 'My saucy bark, inferior far to his,/On your broad main doth wilfully appear'. 'Saucy' here means bold, but also lascivious.

You begin to think that when he writes in Sonnet 76 'O know, sweet love, I always write of you...' he's doing it deliberately to torture his readers, some of whom might have difficulty at this point in suppressing a groan. Can't we have another topic today? But on it goes. In Sonnet 81 Shakespeare writes convincingly 'Your monument shall be my gentle verse', and also 'such virtue hath my pen' which is a boast with an obvious sexual connotation. Yet very soon a note of doubt and even disillusion creeps in: 'I found, or thought I found, you did exceed/The barren tender of a poet's debt' (Sonnet 83). And is it really time to take leave? 'Farewell, thou art too dear for my possessing' (Sonnet 87), though the poet does seem to admit at this late date to a past sexual dimension: 'Thus have I had thee as a dream doth flatter'.

But no, back we are to adoration in Sonnet 91: 'Thy love is better than high birth to me,/Richer than wealth, prouder than garments' cost...' At least Shakespeare pulls out the stops in imagery taken from the natural world. Look at this great last line from Sonnet 94: 'Lilies that fester smell far worse than weeds', an odd, truly memorable image matched in the next

ST JOHN'S COLLEGE CAMBRIDGE

poem, Sonnet 95, with 'a canker in the fragrant rose'. And with 'proud-pied April' in Sonnet 98, conjuring up a splendidly dappled springtime. These poems are marinated in country imagery, but it's not conveyed in any plodding ploughboy's rhyme but in elegant, witty, urban (and urbane) metre. Look at Sonnet 112 in which he coins the highly appropriate and deliciously visual word 'o'ergreen', meaning to cover over, as in re-turfed or re-seeded. Or in which he refers to 'my adder's sense', meaning being as deaf as the adder was reputed to be. The main problem in that poem is its meaning. It is the most obscure of all the Sonnets, and may well have remained unfinished.

It is the continual ingenuity of Shakespeare which strikes the reader. If on occasion there seems to be less evident emotion and more concern for polishing a literary artefact, this is entirely acceptable, given the highly-wrought intellectual nature of the sonnet form. Dazzling wordplay procedes, whether aural punning, as in 'For as you were when first your eye I eyed' (Sonnet 104), or in the subtle alliteration of Sonnet 129. Shakespeare played adroitly with sound, but very rarely at the expense of sense. He was catering to an established taste: the Elizabethans loved verbal rhythms and clever structural wordplay in much the same way that they loved dance and the music of Thomas Tallis and William Byrd.

The interesting thing is that not only was Shakespeare fully aware of the repetitiveness of his task, but that he could turn it almost into a virtue. He knew that it is impossible to keep saying the same thing and also be startlingly original. He admits as much in Sonnet 108, when he compares his litany of love to saying his prayers: 'What's in the brain that ink may character,/Which hath not figured to thee my true spirit?/What's new to speak, what now to register,/That may express my love, or thy dear merit?/Nothing, sweet boy, but yet, like prayers divine,/I must each day say o'er the very same...'

Shakespeare was not too well-bred to indulge a taste for bawdy, with references to sex occurring frequently, in either an overt or covert manner. For instance, Sonnet 109 contains 'in my nature reigned'. 'Nature' was a general term for the genitalia, and this could well be a comic reference to buggery. Whereas Sonnet 107 speaks of an eclipse of the moon, which might be sexual or might refer to the death of Queen Elizabeth, which occurred in 1603, and would if so help to date the poem. Equally it might refer to Elizabeth's sixty-third year, what was called her 'grand climacteric', which occurred in 1596. But this, like so much else, has to remain speculation.

Shakespeare bemoans his lot as an actor, complaining of the sheer vulgarity of it, thus lending support to the theory that the Sonnets were addressed to someone of noble blood. In Sonnet 110 he writes: 'Alas 'tis true, I have gone here and there,/And made myself a motley to the view,/Gored mine own thoughts, sold cheap what is most dear,/Made old offences of affections new.' And again in Sonnet 111 he laments 'public means which public manners breeds'.

Sonnet 116 is perhaps the most admired of the whole collection. It is very moving, no doubt because it is the most absolute in tone. Commencing 'Let me not to the marriage of true minds/Admit impediments', it is a take on the Christian marriage service and is actually often read out at weddings. It is justly famous, and moves through stirring images 'Love's not time's fool, though rosy lips and cheeks/Within his bending sickle's compass come', to an oddly portentous end-couplet. This is a curious mixture of particularity and vagueness: 'If this be error and upon me proved,/I never writ, nor no man ever loved.' But it still sounds magnificent, whatever it may or may not mean.

Sonnet 119 derives its precise metaphors from alchemy (the transmuting of base metal into gold) and medicine, while Sonnet 124 seems surprisingly vague, though the essential meaning that the poet's love does not vary with his beloved's circumstances, is pretty clear. Sonnet 126 is a watershed, the last in the sequence addressed to a man. Those following are mostly addressed to a woman, and Sonnet 127 is the first in praise of a 'black' woman. Black in this sense may mean brunette or ugly, and is certainly meant to indicate a person morally as well as physically dark.

Sonnet 128 refers to a harpsichord (a variety of which was called, incidentally, the virginals) which the poet envies because it gets his mistress' attention. This is a traditional subject for a poem, elaborating on the idea that the lover change places with something inanimate that preoccupies his mistress. The harpsichord is operated by the keys when hit raising wooden jacks which pluck the wires. Shakespeare writes: 'Since saucy jacks so happy are in this,/Give them thy fingers, me thy lips to kiss.' The jumping jacks suggest also a sexual action, and I am reminded of the 20th century bawdy slang rhyme: 'I'm just a jack in the box, with a dose of the pox...'

Sonnet 129 is full of sex. Its message is pretty bleak: 'Th' expense of spirit in a waste of shame/Is lust in action...' It's possible that 'waste of shame' refers to an unwanted pregnancy, or a 'shameful waist', but the main burden of the poem is the sound of panting, of sexual congress, that Shakespeare cleverly injects into the language. 'Past reason hunted, and no sooner had,/Past reason hated....Had, having, and in quest to have.' The repeated 'h' sounds build up to imitate the laboured breathing of coition. Then at the very end comes the moral instruction, or what you might call the anti-moral of the story: 'All this the world well knows, yet none knows

well/To shun the heav'n that leads men to this hell.' Cynical or what?

The next poem, Sonnet 130, beginning 'My mistress' eyes are nothing like the sun', is equally odd but also strangely beguiling. The description is perverse, and some commentators have dismissed it as a winsome trifle, or an attempt to be funny. Perhaps it is a healthy attempt at heightened reality as opposed to the sickening idealization of courtly love. Its invention is impressive, and it rolls majestically to a close. To what kind of woman was it written? Whole books have been devoted to her identity. Sonnet 131 states categorically 'in nothing art thou black save in thy deeds'. In Sonnet 137 Shakespeare implies that she is not exactly faithful, referring to 'the bay where all men ride'.

Sonnet 138, on the other hand, is a masterpiece of sophisticated cynicism. 'When my love swears that she is made of truth,/I do believe her though I know she lies...' it begins, and ends in wordplay and double meaning: 'Therefore I lie with her, and she with me,/And in our faults by lies we flattered be.' Sonnet 144 speaks of 'Two loves I have of comfort and despair', and then becomes more specific. This sounds like autobiography, but probably is no more than a useful poetic opposition. 'The better angel is a man right fair,/The worser spirit a woman coloured ill.' Sonnet 145 has been called the slightest of them all, and some scholars have speculated that it is not even by Shakespeare. However, others have identified a reference to Shakespeare's wife, Anne Hathaway, in the 'hate away' of the penultimate line, which could make it a very early poem and account for its lack of finish.

There is a certain desperation to the tone of the later-numbered Sonnets. In Sonnet 142, Shakespeare says 'Love is my sin', but in 147 he has developed the image to 'My love is as a fever', and 'Past cure I am, now reason is past care...' The infatuation is there, but much darker. 'For I have sworn thee fair, and thought thee bright,/Who art as black as hell, as dark as night.' Sonnet 151 is a phallic-oriented parable, full of erections: 'rising at thy name...To stand in thy affairs....Her love for whose dear love I rise and fall.' But despite its freight of sexual innuendo it begins with words of deep wisdom: 'Love is too young to know what conscience is'.

The last two Sonnets in the collection deal with Cupid and his fire, which seems to refer not only to sexual arousal but also to the perpetual fire of venereal disease. The last line of the last poem, Sonnet 154, reads thus 'Love's fire heats water, water cools not love.' It sounds like a play upon a passage in *The Song of Songs*: 'Many waters cannot quench love, neither can the floods drown it.' But how much these echoes we now find were actually in Shakespeare's mind we can never know. Inevitably, any introduction to the Sonnets is largely conjecture. The reader should draw his or her own portrait of Shakespeare from the material available.

THAMES AT RICHMOND FROM THE TERRACE

LATER LIFE

In 1594 Shakespeare the actor and theatre-writer threw in his lot with the Lord Chamberlain's Men, with whom he stayed for the rest of his career. A company of actors then consisted of between eight and twelve players who each invested in the enterprise and became shareholders, employing other men as and when the occasion demanded. The system suited Shakespeare, who made money as the best writer around, and as shareholder. He prospered and lived mainly in London. He probably visited Stratford often, to see to his affairs and visit his family. In 1597 his financial situation was so good that he could purchase Stratford's finest house, New Place. At the end of 1598 the company's lease on the Shoreditch site of the Theatre expired, and at Christmas-time the shareholders removed the timber of the old construction, which was rightfully theirs, and transported it across the river to build the Globe at Southwark.

Shakespeare's earlier plays were written mainly in verse, often in rhyme, though the comic characters tended to be in prose. His middle period was mostly in prose, and the late work moved into a new, deeper poetry. In terms of linear development it was a move from lyric poetry to dramatic prose, and then into dramatic poetry. He achieved much (just consider the roll-call of his creations, which includes *A Midsummer Night's Dream, Hamlet, Macbeth, King Lear, Othello*, the History plays and *The Tempest*), even though plays were not at that time considered to be serious literature. They were not sacrosanct texts like Beckett's or Pinter's, each comma or pause weighed to exquisite point and precision, but were there to be corrected and augmented, ultimately to be acted. They were a rough guide only, not an A-Z.

It should be noted in passing that Shakespeare's words would not have sounded in his own day as we speak them today. For a start, nobody drank water (it had a tendency to kill if taken internally; few ventured to use it externally either), and tea had not yet arrived in England. Ale was the standard drink, and you started with it at breakfast. As a result, passions ran higher: people sang and quarrelled openly in the street, and gave themselves more readily to emotion. So there would be less subtlety than dramatic bombast put into the speaking of Shakespeare's phrases. In addition, the accent was very different from what we hear today. Anthony Burgess estimated it thus: part Lancashire, part New England and part Dublin. It would certainly sound much broader, more American, than London English in the late 20th century.

In 1623 the First Folio of Shakespeare's plays was collected, edited and published by his friends Heminges and Condell, containing thirty-six works. Scholars now attribute thirty-eight or thirty-nine plays to him. Shakespeare was above all a professional, the reliable supplier of actable plays, who could please the groundlings (those who could only afford to stand to see the plays), the apprentices and the courtly wits as well. But just because he could turn out two plays a year, he should never be undervalued. The qualities of wisdom and compassion he possessed are rare. He was the great poet of the Elizabethan literary renaissance, and remains the greatest all-round writer in the English language.

Shakespeare was quintessentially bourgeois, but he was a great dramatic poet rather than a literary tradesman. People say of him, as they do of Dickens, that he would have written for TV had he lived today. Well, perhaps so, but it would have been the highest order of writing in comparison to the generality of feeble stuff foisted upon us nowadays. He always wanted to be a gentleman, and in 1599 finally received his armorial bearings from the Garter King-of-Arms. The motto was *Non Sans Droict*, or 'Not Without Right', which Ben Jonson later cruelly parodied as 'Not Without Mustard'.

Shakespeare retired to Stratford in his 40s, to enjoy the fruits of a lifetime's hard work. After about 1609, it appears that his reputation was in question. Rumour circulated that he actually wasn't very clever, and that he wrote too easily (and therefore not profoundly); also people began to say

THE THAMES NEAR WINDSOR

that he wasn't in the height of fashion. Well, Shakespeare's light may then have been briefly shrouded, but he has since proved himself well beyond the reach of fashion.

He seems never to have come to terms with his son's death. Hamnet died - we don't know how - in 1596 at the age of eleven. Two of Shakespeare's brothers, Gilbert and Richard, were unmarried and died childless. The third and youngest, Edmund, had a bastard, but both father and son died young. Shakespeare was obsessed with inheritance, but had no male heir to carry forward the family name. This was evidently an enormous blow to him. In later life he wrote increasingly about suffering, with an insider's knowledge of intense grief.

In his will, he famously left 'unto my wife my second best bed'. Given the complex legal implications of bequests at that time, we simply don't know the real significance of this act. It might indicate that he disliked or distrusted his wife, and it might not. But inevitably it continues to have an emotional resonance for us. It is perhaps revealing that he didn't leave any jewel or keepsake to his wife. But then he never mentions books either, of which you might suppose he had a substantial collection of some value. We know that he did bequeath the majority of his property, including a house in Blackfriars, to his eldest daughter Susanna.

ENGLISH PASTORAL SCENE

William Shakespeare died in 1616, aged 52, on 23rd April. It seems likely that he died of typhoid rather than the plague which killed so many. Evidence suggests that in those days before people knew how typhoid was carried he could have been poisoned by the filthy stream that ran close to his distinguished home. The 'Sweet Swan of Avon', as his friend and fellow dramatist Ben Jonson called him, was no more. Luckily his writings, full of dangerous subtlety and bewitchment, are with us still.

CONCLUSION

Shakespeare makes the point time and again in the Sonnets that long after he is dead, these lines will still be read. That, in effect, his work will be immortal. There is no false modesty about this, though he sometimes pretends that he wishes his beloved's beauty would live on in place of his words. Shakespeare had the rare ability not only to encapsulate the spirit of his own age but to render his shrewd observations in timeless statements. We read him today as he has always been read: for enjoyment, for enlightenment, for education and for entertainment.

The original Globe theatre was burnt to the ground in 1613 during a performance of *Henry VIII*, miraculously with no loss of life. That site is now mostly under Southwark Bridge Road and Anchor Terrace, the final approach to the Bridge itself. In 1997, thanks to the untiring efforts of the actor Sam Wanamaker, a full-size replica of the polygonal Globe was opened close to the original site on Bankside, to great popular acclaim. Shakespeare's plays are re-enacted there during the summer, largely in the open air. Bear-pits and brothels may no longer enliven the locality, but the spirit of Shakespeare has taken triumphant re-possession.

THE THAMES AT ETON

Each age adapts Shakespeare to its own needs, and interprets his work in the light of its values. The 20th century has been particularly rich in interpretations, and there seems to be more interest now in the Bard than ever before. Historians have done ground-breaking work on the social context of his times, and we will perhaps understand more about the man as further scraps of information are uncovered. Different interpretations will never harm him because Shakespeare's genius is large enough to contain them all and still retain its distinctive character.

In the south aisle of the nave of Southwark Cathedral an alabaster effigy of William Shakespeare reclines in a recess. When I last visited it, someone had planted a sprig of rosemary in its fist with a little earth stuffed into the hollow between the fingers. Was this entirely by design? (The significance of rosemary in Shakespeare's time is interesting: it was tied to boys' sleeves at weddings to symbolize fidelity.) This stone memorial was paid for by public subscription and dedicated in 1911. The Cathedral was Shakespeare's parish church, St Saviour's as it was known then, and he would have worshipped there on occasion. Certainly his brother Edmund, an actor also, was buried there aged twenty-seven in an unmarked grave. There is a tradition that Shakespeare paid for the Great Bell to be tolled at the service. Edmund is now commemorated by an inscribed stone in the paving of the Choir.

JB Priestley rightly characterized Shakespeare's writing as 'pictorial mode of thought and communication'. This might supply one reason why his work has survived so successfully. We live in an increasingly media-dominated age, in which all the major stimuli are visual: advertising, TV and film have been supplemented by interactive computer graphics, and 24 hour news coverage. Where do books stand in amongst these statistics? Apparently, they are selling better than ever, even if no one reads them. So if the worst comes to the worst and literature is marginalized, there will always be an appetite for good visual stories which can be adapted for film or TV. Shakespeare's stories will continue to be plundered in this way - shamelessly rewritten and hashed up - because their inner truth is timeless. William Shakespeare, out of the profound understanding of an exceptional heart coupled with a well-stocked mind, wrote words and made myths which are eternal.

Towards the end of 1998 a film about Shakespeare's love life was released in America, directed by John Madden. Called *Shakespeare in Love*, it was scripted by Marc Norman and Tom Stoppard, and the identity of the Dark Lady was revealed in the fair form of Gwyneth Paltrow. Shakespeare himself was played by Joseph Fiennes. The critics poured praise upon it - it was romantic, mischievous, enchanting. The book of the film featured a selection of the Bard's love lyrics, including sixteen of the Sonnets.

Apparently the impetus behind the film, aside from any merely commercial consideration, was to make the writer more human, to bring him to life. But was this necessary? Shakespeare is the most human of great writers and the most alive today. Any popular filmic tribute to the Bard is bound to run the risk of being too flippant or too cute. Only the great Orson Welles achieved something both intelligent and respectful (also deeply affectionate) in his version of the Falstaff story, *Chimes at Midnight* (1966).

We perhaps do best not to pry too closely into Shakespeare's life. He was buried on 25 April 1616 in Holy Trinity Church in Stratford where he had been christened. Perhaps he himself penned the following inscription above the grave:

Good friend, for Jesus' sake forbear

To dig the dust enclosed here.

Blessed be the man that spares these stones

And cursed be he that moves my bones.

It's no longer the time to wash his dirty laundry in public. Let him rest. And let us return to the great glories of his writing.

1

From fairest creatures we desire increase,
That thereby beauty's rose might never die,
But as the riper should by time decease,
His tender heir might bear his memory:
But thou, contracted to thine own bright eyes,
Feed'st thy light's flame with self-substantial fuel,
Making a famine where abundance lies,
Thyself thy foe, to thy sweet self too cruel.
Thou that art now the world's fresh ornament,
And only herald to the gaudy spring,
Within thine own bud buriest thy content,
And, tender churl, makest waste in niggarding.
   Pity the world, or else this glutton be,
    To eat the world's due, by the grave and thee.

2

When forty winters shall besiege thy brow,
And dig deep trenches in thy beauty's field,
Thy youth's proud livery; so gazed on now,
Will be a totter'd weed, of small worth held:
Then being asked, where all thy beauty lies,
Where all the treasure of thy lusty days;
To say, within thine own deep-sunken eyes,
Were an all-eating shame and thriftless praise.
How much more praise deserved thy beauty's use,
If thou couldst answer, 'This fair child of mine
Shall sum my count, and make my old excuse,'
Proving his beauty by succession thine!
   This were to be new made when thou art old,
    And see thy blood warm when thou feel'st it cold.

3

Look in thy glass, and tell the face thou viewest
Now is the time that face should form another;
Whose fresh repair if now thou not renewest,
Thou dost beguile the world, unbless some mother.
For where is she so fair whose unear'd womb
Disdains the tillage of thy husbandry?
Or who is he so fond will be the tomb
Of his self-love, to stop posterity?
Thou art thy mother's glass, and she in thee
Calls back the lovely April of her prime:
So thou through windows of thine age shalt see,
Despite of wrinkles, this thy golden time.
   But if thou live, remember'd not to be,
    Die single, and thine image dies with thee.

4

Unthrifty loveliness, why dost thou spend
Upon thyself thy beauty's legacy?
Nature's bequest gives nothing, but doth lend;
And, being frank, she lends to those are free.
Then, beauteous niggard, why dost thou abuse
The bounteous largess given thee to give?
Profitless usurer, why dost thou use
So great a sum of sums, yet canst not live?
For having traffic with thyself alone,
Thou of thyself thy sweet self dost deceive.
Then how, when nature calls thee to be gone,
What acceptable audit canst thou leave?
   Thy unused beauty must be tomb'd with thee,
   Which, used, lives th' executor to be.

5

Those hours, that with gentle work did frame
The lovely gaze where every eye doth dwell,
Will play the tyrants to the very same,
And that unfair which fairly doth excel:
For never-resting time leads summer on
To hideous winter and confounds him there;
Sap checked with frost, and lusty leaves quite gone,
Beauty o'ersnow'd, and bareness everywhere:
Then, were not summer's distillation left,
A liquid prisoner pent in walls of glass,
Beauty's effect with beauty were bereft,
Nor it, nor no remembrance what it was:
   But flowers distill'd, though they with winter meet,
   Leese but their show; their substance still lives sweet.

6

Then let not winter's ragged hand deface
In thee thy summer, ere thou be distill'd:
Make sweet some vial; treasure thou some place
With beauty's treasure, ere it be self-kill'd.
That use is not forbidden usury,
Which happies those that pay the willing loan;
That's for thyself to breed another thee,
Or ten times happier, be it ten for one;
Ten times thyself were happier than thou art,
If ten of thine ten times refigured thee:
Then what could death do, if thou shouldst depart,
Leaving thee living in posterity?
   Be not self-will'd, for thou art much too fair
   To be death's conquest and make worms thine heir.

7

Lo, in the orient when the gracious light
Lifts up his burning head, each under eye
Doth homage to his new-appearing sight,
Serving with looks his sacred majesty;
And having climb'd the steep-up heavenly hill,
Resembling strong youth in his middle age,
Yet mortal looks adore his beauty still,
Attending on his golden pilgrimage;
But when from highmost pitch, with weary car,
Like feeble age, he reeleth from the day,
The eyes, ('fore duteous), now converted are
From his low tract and look another way:
   So thou, thyself outgoing in thy noon,
   Unlooked on diest, unless thou get a son.

8

Music to hear, why hear'st thou music sadly?
Sweets with sweets war not, joy delights in joy.
Why lov'st thou that which thou receiv'st not gladly,
Or else receivest with pleasure thine annoy?
If the true concord of well-tuned sounds,
By unions married, do offend thine ear,
They do but sweetly chide thee, who confounds
In singleness the parts that thou shouldst bear
Mark how one string, sweet husband to another,
Strikes each in each by mutual ordering;
Resembling sire and child and happy mother,
Who, all in one, one pleasing note do sing:
    Whose speechless song, being many, seeming one,
    Sings this to thee, 'Thou single wilt prove none.'

9

Is it for fear to wet a widow's eye
That thou consum' st thyself in single life?
Ah! if thou issueless shalt hap to die,
The world will wail thee, like a makeless wife;
The world will be thy widow, and still weep
That thou no form of thee hast left behind,
When every private widow well may keep,
By children's eyes her husband's shape in mind.
Look, what an unthrift in the world doth spend
Shifts but his place for still the world enjoys it;
But beauty's waste hath in the world an end,
And kept unused, the user so destroys it.
    No love toward others in that bosom sits
    That on himself such murd'rous shame commits.

10

For shame deny that thou bear'st love to any,
Who for thyself art so unprovident.
Grant, if thou wilt, thou art belov'd of many,
But that thou none lov'st is most evident;
For thou art so possessed with murd'rous hate,
That 'gainst thyself thou stick'st not to conspire,
Seeking that beauteous roof to ruinate,
Which to repair should be thy chief desire.
O, change thy thought, that I may change my mind!
Shall hate be fairer lodged than gentle love?
Be, as thy presence is, gracious and kind,
Or to thyself, at least, kind-hearted prove:
    Make thee another self, for love of me,
    That beauty still may live in thine or thee.

11

As fast as thou shalt wane, so fast thou grow'st
In one of thine, from that which thou departest;
And that fresh blood which youngly thou bestow'st
Thou mayst call thine when thou from youth convertest.
Herein lives wisdom, beauty, and increase;
Without this, folly, age, and cold decay:
If all were minded so, the times should cease,
And threescore year would make the world away,
Let those whom Nature hath not made for store,
Harsh, featureless, and rude, barrenly perish:
Look, whom she best endow'd she gave the more;
Which bounteous gift thou shouldst in bounty cherish:
    She carved thee for her seal, and meant thereby
    Thou shouldst print more, not let that copy die.

12

When I do count the clock that tells the time,
And see the brave day sunk in hideous night;
When I behold the violet past prime,
And sable curls all silver'd o'er with white;
When lofty trees I see barren of leaves,
Which erst from heat did canopy the herd,
And summer's green, all girded up in sheaves,
Borne on the bier with white and bristly beard;
Then of thy beauty do I question make,
That thou among the wastes of time must go,
Since sweets and beauties do themselves forsake,
And die as fast as they see others grow;
   And nothing 'gainst Time's scythe can make defence
   Save breed to brave him when he takes thee hence.

13

O that you were yourself! but, love, you are
No longer yours than you yourself here live:
Against this coming end you should prepare,
And your sweet semblance to some other give.
So should that beauty which you hold in lease
Find no determination; then you were
Yourself again, after your self's decease,
When your sweet issue your sweet form should bear
Who lets so fair a house fall to decay,
Which husbandry in honour might uphold
Against the stormy gusts of winter's day
And barren rage of death's eternal cold?
   O, none but unthrifts: dear my love, you know
   You had a father; let your son say so.

14

Not from the stars do I my judgement pluck;
And yet methinks I have astronomy,
But not to tell of good or evil luck,
Of plagues, of dearths, or seasons' quality;
Nor can I fortune to brief minutes tell,
Pointing to each his thunder, rain, and wind,
Or say with princes if it shall go well,
By oft predict that I in heaven find:
But from thine eyes my knowledge I derive,
And, constant stars, in them I read such art,
As truth and beauty shall together thrive,
If from thyself to store thou wouldst convert;
   Or else of thee this I prognosticate:
   Thy end is truth's and beauty's doom and date.

15

When I consider every thing that grows
Holds in perfection but a little moment,
That this huge stage presenteth naught but shows
Whereon the stars in secret influence comment;
When I perceive that men as plants increase,
Cheered and checked even by the self-same sky,
Vaunt in their youthful sap, at height decrease,
And wear their brave state out of memory;
Then the conceit of this inconstant stay
Sets you most rich in youth before my sight,
Where wasteful Time debateth with decay,
To change your day of youth to sullied night;
   And, all in war with Time, for love of you,
   As he takes from you, I engraft you new.

16

But wherefore do not you a mightier way
Make war upon this bloody tyrant, Time?
And fortify yourself in your decay
With means more blessed than my barren rhyme?
Now stand you on the top of happy hours;
And many maiden gardens, yet unset,
With virtuous wish would bear your living flowers,
Much liker than your painted counterfeit:
So should the lines of life that life repair,
Which this, Time's pencil, or my pupil pen,
Neither in inward worth nor outward fair,
Can make you live yourself in eyes of men.
    To give away yourself keeps yourself still:
    And you must live, drawn by your own sweet skill.

18

Shall I compare thee to a summer's day?
Thou art more lovely and more temperate:
Rough winds do shake the darling buds of May,
And summer's lease hath all to short a date:
Sometime too hot the eye of heaven shines,
And often is his gold complexion dimm'd;
And every fair from fair sometime declines,
By chance, or nature's changing course, untrimm'd;
But thy eternal summer shall not fade,
Nor lose possession of that fair thou ow'st;
Nor shall Death brag thou wand'rest in his shade,
When in eternal lines to time thou grow'st;
    So long as men can breathe, or eyes can see,
    So long lives this, and this gives life to thee.

17

Who will believe my verse in time to come,
If it were fill'd with your most high deserts?
Though yet, heaven knows, it is but as a tomb
Which hides your life, and shows not half your parts.
If I could write the beauty of your eyes,
And in fresh numbers number all your graces,
The age to come would say, 'This poet lies,
Such heavenly touches ne'er touched earthly faces.'
So should my papers, yellow'd with their age,
Be scorn'd, like old men of less truth than tongue;
And your true rights be term'd a poet's rage,
And stretched metre of an antique song:
    But were some child of yours alive that time,
    You should live twice, in it and in my rhyme.

19

Devouring Time, blunt thou the lion's paws,
And make the earth devour her own sweet brood;
Pluck the keen teeth from the fierce tiger's jaws,
And burn the long-lived phoenix in her blood;
Make glad and sorry seasons as thou fleet'st
And do whate'er thou wilt, swift-footed Time,
To the wide world and all her fading sweets;
But I forbid thee one most heinous crime:
O, carve not with thy hours my love's fair brow,
Nor draw no lines there with thine antique pen;
Him in thy course untainted do allow
For beauty's pattern to succeeding men.
    Yet, do thy worst, old Time; despite thy wrong,
    My love shall in my verse ever live young.

20

A woman's face, with Nature's own hand painted,
Hast thou, the master-mistress of my passion;
A woman's gentle heart, but not acquainted
With shifting change, as is false women's fashion;
An eye more bright than theirs, less false in rolling,
Gilding the object whereupon it gazeth;
A man in hue all hues in his controlling,
Which steals men's eyes, and women's souls amazeth.
And for a woman wert thou first created:
Till Nature, as she wrought thee, fell a-doting,
And by addition me of thee defeated,
By adding one thing to my purpose nothing.
    But since she pricked thee out out for women's pleasure,
    Mine be thy love, and thy love's use their treasure.

21

So is it not with me as with that Muse
Stirr'd by a painted beauty to his verse,
Who heaven itself for ornament doth use,
And every fair with his fair doth rehearse;
Making a couplement of proud compare,
With sun and moon, with earth and sea's rich gems,
With April's first-born flowers, and all things rare
That heaven's air in this huge rondure hems.
O, let me, true in love, but truly write,
And then believe me, my love is as fair
As any mother's child, though not so bright
As those gold candles fixed in heaven's air:
    Let them say more that like of hearsay well;
    I will not praise that purpose not to sell.

22

My glass shall not persuade me I am old,
So long as youth and thou are of one date;
But when in thee time's furrows I behold,
Then look I death my days should expiate.
For all that beauty that doth cover thee
Is but the seemly raiment of my heart,
Which in my breast doth live, as thine in me:
How can I, then, be elder than thou art?
O, therefore, love, be of thyself so wary
As I, not for myself, but for thee will;
Bearing thy heart, which I will keep so chary
As tender nurse her babe from faring ill.
    Presume not on thy heart when mine is slain;
    Thou gav'st me thine, not to give back again.

DANCING ON A SUMMER'S DAY

23

As an unperfect actor on the stage,
Who, with his fear is put besides his part,
Or some fierce thing replete with too much rage,
Whose strength's abundance weakens his own heart;
So I, for fear of trust, forget to say
The perfect ceremony of love's rite,
And in mine own love's strength seem to decay,
O'ercharged with burthen of mine own love's might.
O, let my books be, then, the eloquence
And dumb presagers of my speaking breast;
Who plead for love, and look for recompense,
More than that tongue that more hath more expressed.
    O, learn to read what silent love hath writ:
    To hear with eyes belongs to love's fine wit.

24

Mine eye hath play'd the painter, and hath stell'd
Thy beauty's form in table of my heart,
My body is the frame wherein 'tis held,
And perspective it is best painter's art.
For through the painter must you see his skill,
To find where your true image pictured lies;
Which in my bosom's shop is hanging still,
That hath his windows glazed with thine eyes.
Now see what good turns eyes for eyes have done:
Mine eyes have drawn thy shape, and thine for me
Are windows to my breast, where-through the sun
Delights to peep, to gaze therein on thee;
    Yet eyes this cunning want to grace their art,
    They draw but what they see, know not the heart.

25

Let those who are in favour with their stars
Of public honour and proud titles boast,
Whilst I, whom fortune of such triumph bars,
Unlooked for joy in that I honour most.
Great princes' favourites their fair leaves spread
But as the marigold at the sun's eye;
And in themselves their pride lies buried,
For at a frown they in their glory die.
The painful warrior famoused for fight,
After a thousand victories once foil'd,
Is from the book of honour razed quite,
And all the rest forgot for which he toil'd:
    Then happy I, that love and am beloved
    Where I may not remove nor be removed.

26

Lord of my love, to whom in vassalage
Thy merit hath my duty strongly knit,
To thee I send this written ambassage,
To witness duty, not to show my wit:
Duty so great, which wit so poor as mine
May make seem bare, in wanting words to show it,
But that I hope some good conceit of thine
In thy soul's thought, all naked, will bestow it;
Till whatsoever star that guides my moving,
Points on me graciously with fair aspect,
And puts apparel on my totter'd loving,
To show me worthy of thy sweet respect:
    Then may I dare to boast how I do love thee;
    Till then not show my head where thou mayst prove me.

28

How can I, then, return in happy plight,
That am debarr'd the benefit of rest?
When day's oppression is not eased by night,
But day by night, and night by day, oppressed?
And each, though enemies to either's reign,
Do in consent shake hands to torture me;
The one by toil, the other to complain
How far I toil, still farther off from thee.
I tell the day, to please him thou art bright,
And dost him grace when clouds do blot the heaven:
So flatter I the swart-complexion'd night,
When sparkling stars twire not thou gild'st the even.
　　But day doth daily draw my sorrows longer,
　　And night doth nightly make grief's strength seem stronger.

27

Weary with toil, I haste me to my bed,
The dear repose for limbs with travel tired;
But then begins a journey in my head,
To work my mind, when body's work's expired:
For then my thoughts, from far where I abide,
Intend a zealous pilgrimage to thee,
And keep my drooping eyelids open wide,
Looking on darkness which the blind do see:
Save that my soul's imaginary sight
Presents thy shadow to my sightless view,
Which, like a jewel hung in ghastly night,
Makes black night beauteous, and her old face new.
　　Lo, thus, by day my limbs, by night my mind,
　　For thee and for myself no quiet find.

29

When, in disgrace with fortune and men's eyes,
I all alone beweep my outcast state,
And trouble deaf heaven with my bootless cries,
And look upon myself, and curse my fate,
Wishing me like to one more rich in hope,
Featured like him, like him with friends possessed,
Desiring this man's art, and that man's scope,
With what I most enjoy contented least;
Yet in these thoughts myself almost despising,
Haply I think on thee,—and then my state,
Like to the lark at break of day arising
From sullen earth, sings hymns at heaven's gate;
　　For thy sweet love remember'd, such wealth brings,
　　That then I scorn to change my state with kings.

30

When to the sessions of sweet silent thought
I summon up remembrance of things past,
I sigh the lack of many a thing I sought,
And with old woes new wail my dear time's waste.
Then can I drown an eye, unused to flow,
For precious friends hid in death's dateless night,
And weep afresh love's long-since-cancell'd woe,
And moan the expense of many a vanished sight:
Then can I grieve at grievances foregone,
And heavily from woe to woe tell o'er
The sad account of fore-bemoaned moan,
Which I new pay as if not paid before.
    But if the while I think on thee, dear friend.
    All losses are restored, and sorrows end.

31

Thy bosom is endeared with all hearts,
Which I by lacking have supposed dead;
And there reigns love, and all love's loving parts,
And all those friends which I thought buried.
How many a holy and obsequious tear
Hath dear religious love stol'n from mine eye,
As interest of the dead, which now appear
But things removed, that hidden in thee lie!
Thou art the grave where buried love doth live,
Hung with the trophies of my lovers gone,
Who all their parts of me to thee did give;
That due of many now is thine alone:
    Their images I loved I view in thee,
    And thou, all they, hast all the all of me.

32

If thou survive my well-contented day,
When that churl Death my bones with dust shall cover,
And shalt by fortune once more re-survey
These poor rude lines of thy deceased lover:
Compare them with the bettering of the time,
And though they be outstripped by every pen,
Reserve them for my love, not for their rhyme,
Exceeded by the height of happier men.
O, then vouchsafe me but this loving thought:
Had my friend's Muse grown with this growing age,
A dearer birth than this his love had brought,
To march in ranks of better equipage:
    But since he died, and poets better prove,
    Theirs for their style I'll read, his for his love.

33

Full many a glorious morning have I seen
Flatter the mountain-tops with sovereign eye,
Kissing with golden face the meadows green,
Gilding pale streams with heavenly alchemy;
Anon permit the basest clouds to ride
With ugly rack on his celestial face,
And from the forlorn world his visage hide,
Stealing unseen to west with this disgrace:
Even so my sun one early morn did shine
With all-triumphant splendour on my brow;
But, out, alack! he was but one hour mine,
The region cloud hath masked him from me now.
    Yet him for this my love no whit disdaineth;
    Suns of the world may stain when heaven's sun staineth.

34

Why didst thou promise such a beauteous day,
And make me travel forth without my cloak,
To let base clouds o'ertake me in my way,
Hiding thy bravery in their rotten smoke?
'Tis not enough that through the cloud thou break,
To dry the rain on my storm-beaten face,
For no man well of such a salve can speak,
That heals the wound, and cures not the disgrace:
Nor can thy shame give physic to my grief;
Though thou repent, yet I have still the loss:
The offender's sorrow lends but weak relief
To him that bears the strong offence's cross.
    Ah, but those tears are pearl which thy love sheeds,
    And they are rich, and ransom all ill deeds.

35

No more be grieved at that which thou hast done:
Roses have thorns, and silver fountains mud;
Clouds and eclipses stain both moon and sun,
And loathsome canker lives in sweetest bud.
All men make faults, and even I in this,
Authorizing thy trespass with compare,
Myself corrupting, salving thy amiss,
Excusing thy sins more than thy sins are;
For to thy sensual fault I bring in sense,–
Thy adverse party is thy advocate,–
And 'gainst myself a lawful plea commence:
Such civil war is in my love and hate,
    That I an accessary needs must be
    To that sweet thief which sourly robs from me.

36

Let me confess that we two must be twain,
Although our undivided loves are one:
So shall those blots that do with me remain,
Without thy help, by me be borne alone.
In our two loves there is but one respect,
Though in our lives a separable spite,
Which though it alter not love's sole effect,
Yet doth it steal sweet hours from love's delight.
I may not evermore acknowledge thee,
Lest my bewailed guilt should do thee shame;
Nor thou with public kindness honour me;
Unless thou take that honour from thy name:
    But do not so; I love thee in such sort,
    As, thou being mine, mine is thy good report.

37

As a decrepit father takes delight
To see his active child do deeds of youth;
So I, made lame by Fortune's dearest spite,
Take all my comfort of thy worth and truth;
For whether beauty, birth, or, wealth, or wit,:
Or any of these all, or all, or more,
Entitled in their parts do crowned sit,
I make my love engrafted to this store:
So then I am not lame, poor, nor despised,
Whilst that this shadow doth such substance give,
That I in thy abundance am sufficed,
And by a part of all thy glory live.
　　Look; what is best, that best I wish in thee:
　　This wish I have; then ten times happy me!

38

How can my Muse want subject to invent,
While thou dost breathe, that pour'st into my verse
Thine own sweet argument, too excellent
For ever vulgar paper to rehearse?
O, give thyself the thanks, if aught in me
Worthy perusal stand against thy sight;
For who's so dumb that cannot write to thee,
When thou thyself dost give invention light?
Be thou the tenth Muse, ten times more in worth
Than those old nine which rhymers invocate;
And he that calls on thee, let him bring forth
Eternal numbers to outlive long date.
　　If my slight Muse do please these curious days,
　　The pain be mine, but thine shall be the praise.

39

O, how thy worth with manners may I sing,
When thou art all the better part of me?
What can mine own praise to mine own self bring?
And what is't but mine own when I praise thee?
Even for this let us divided live,
And our dear love lose name of single one,
That by this separation I may give
That due to thee which thou deservest alone.
O absence, what a torment wouldst thou prove,
Were it not thy sour leisure gave sweet leave
To entertain the time with thoughts of love,
Which time and thoughts so sweetly doth deceive,
　　And that thou teachest how to make one twain,
　　By praising him here who doth hence remain!

40

Take all my loves, my love, yea, take them all;
What hast thou then more than thou hadst before?
No love, my love, that thou mayst true love call;
All mine was thine before thou hadst this more.
Then, if for my love thou my love receivest,
I cannot blame thee for my love thou usest;
But yet be blamed, if thou this self deceivest
By wilful taste of what thyself refusest.
I do forgive thy robbery, gentle thief,
Although thou steal thee all my poverty;
And yet, love knows, it is a greater grief
To bear love's wrong than hate's known injury.
　　Lascivious grace, in whom all ill well shows,
　　Kill me with spites; yet we must not be foes.

41

Those pretty wrongs that liberty commits
When I am sometime absent from thy heart
Thy beauty and thy years full well befits,
For still temptation follows where thou art.
Gentle thou art, and therefore to be won,
Beauteous thou art, therefore to be assailed;
And when a woman woos, what woman's son
Will sourly leave her till he have prevailed?
Ay me! but yet thou mightst my seat forbear,
And chide thy beauty and thy straying youth,
Who lead thee in their riot even there
Where thou art forced to break a twofold truth,–
   Hers, by thy beauty tempting her to thee,
   Thine, by thy beauty being false to me.

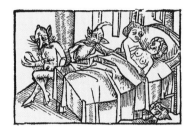

42

That thou hast her, it is not all my grief,
And yet it may be said I loved her dearly;
That she hath thee, is of my wailing chief,
A loss in love that touches me more nearly.
Loving offenders, thus I will excuse ye:–
Thou dost love her, because thou know'st I love her;
And for my sake even so doth she abuse me,
Suff'ring my friend for my sake to approve her.
If I lose thee, my loss is my love's gain,
And losing her, my friend hath found that loss;
Both find each other, and I lose both twain,
And both for my sake lay on me this cross:
   But here's the joy; my friend and I are one;
   Sweet flattery! then she loves but me alone.

43

When most I wink, then do mine eyes best see,
For all the day they view things unrespected;
But when I sleep, in dreams they look on thee,
And, darkly bright, are bright in dark directed.
Then thou, whose shadow shadows doth make bright,
How would thy shadow's form form happy show
To the clear day with thy much clearer light,
When to unseeing eyes thy shade shines so!
How would, I say, mine eyes be blessed made
By looking on thee in the living day,
When in dead night thy fair imperfect shade
Through heavy sleep on sightless eyes doth stay!
   All days are nights to see till I see thee,
   And nights bright days when dreams do show thee me.

44

If the dull substance of my flesh were thought,
Injurious distance should not stop my way;
For then, despite of space, I would be brought,
From limits far remote, where thou dost stay.
No matter then although my foot did stand
Upon the farthest earth removed from thee;
For nimble thought can jump both sea and land,
As soon as think the place where he would be.
But, ah, thought kills me, that I am not thought,
To leap large lengths of miles when thou art gone,
But that, so much of earth and water wrought,
I must attend time's leisure with my moan.
    Receiving naught by elements so slow
    But heavy tears, badges of either's woe.

45

The other two, slight air and purging fire,
Are both with thee, wherever I abide;
The first my thought, the other my desire,
These present-absent with swift motion slide.
For when these quicker elements are gone
In tender embassy of love to thee,
My life, being made of four, with two alone
Sinks down to death, oppressed with melancholy;
Until life's composition be recured
By those swift messengers return'd from thee,
Who even but now come back again, assured
Of thy fair health, recounting it to me:
    This told, I joy; but then no longer glad,
    I send them back again, and straight grow sad.

46

Mine eye and heart are at a mortal war,
How to divide the conquest of thy sight;
Mine eye my heart thy picture's sight would bar,
My heart mine eye the freedom of that right.
My heart doth plead that thou in him dost lie–
A closet never pierced with crystal eyes–
But the defendant doth that plea deny,
And says in him thy fair appearance lies.
To 'cide this title is impannelled
A quest of thoughts, all tenants to the heart;
And by their verdict is determined
The clear eye's moiety and the dear heart's part:
    As thus; mine eye's due is thy outward part,
    And my heart's right thy inward love of heart.

47

Betwixt mine eye and heart a league is took,
And each doth good turns now unto the other;
When that mine eye is famished for a look,
Or heart in love with sighs himself doth smother,
With my love's picture then my eye doth feast,
And to be painted banquet bids my heart;
Another time mine eye is my heart's guest,
And in his thoughts of love doth share a part:
So, either by thy picture or my love,
Thyself away are present still with me;
For thou no farther than my thoughts canst move,
And I am still with them, and they with thee;
    Or, if they sleep, thy picture in my sight
    Awakes my heart to heart's and eye's delight.

48

How careful was I, when I took my way,
Each trifle under truest bars to thrust,
That to my use it might unused stay
From hands of falsehood, in sure wards of trust!
But thou, to whom my jewels trifles are,
Most worthy comfort, now my greatest grief,
Thou, best of dearest, and mine only care,
Art left the prey of every vulgar thief.
Thee have I not locked up in any chest,
Save where thou art not, though I feel thou art,
Within the gentle closure of my breast,
From whence at pleasure thou mayst come and part;
    And even thence thou wilt be stol'n, I fear,
    For truth proves thievish for a prize so dear.

49

Against that time, if ever that time come,
When I shall see thee frown on my defects,
Whenas thy love hath cast his utmost sum,
Call'd to that audit by advised respects;
Against that time when thou shalt strangely pass,
And scarcely greet me with that sun, thine eye,
When love, converted from the thing it was,
Shall reasons find of settled gravity;
Against that time do I ensconce me here
Within the knowledge of mine own desert,
And this my hand against myself uprear,
To guard the lawful reasons on thy part:
    To leave poor me thou hast the strength of laws,
    Since why to love I can allege no cause.

50

How heavy do I journey on the way,
When what I seek—my weary travel's end –
Doth teach that ease and that repose to say,
Thus far miles are measured from thy friend!
The beast that bears me, tired with my woe,
Plods dully on, to bear that weight in me,
As if by some instinct the wretch did know
His rider loved not speed, being made from thee:
The bloody spur cannot provoke him on
That sometimes anger thrusts into his hide;
Which heavily he answers with a groan,
More sharp to me than spurring to his side;
    For that same groan doth put this in my mind;
    My grief lies onward, and my joy behind.

51

Thus can my love excuse the slow offence
Of my dull bearer when from thee I speed:
From where thou art why should I haste me thence?
Till I return, of posting is no need.
O, what excuse will my poor beast then find,
When swift extremity can seem but slow?
Then should I spur, though mounted on the wind,
In winged speed no motion shall I know:
Then can no horse with my desire keep pace;
Therefore desire, of perfect'st love being made,
Shall neigh no dull flesh in his fiery race;
But love, for love, thus shall excuse my jade,
   Since from thee going he went wilful slow,
   Towards thee I'll run, and give him leave to go.

52

So am I as the rich, whose blessed key
Can bring him to his sweet up-locked treasure,
The which he will not every hour survey,
For blunting the fine point of seldom pleasure.
Therefore are feasts so solemn and so rare,
Since, seldom coming, in the long year set,
Like stones of worth they thinly placed are,
Or captain jewels in the carcanet.
So is the time that keeps you, as my chest,
Or as the wardrobe which the robe doth hide,
To make some special instant special blest,
By new unfolding his imprison'd pride.
   Blessed are you, whose worthiness gives scope,
   Being had, to triumph, being lacked, to hope.

53

What is your substance, whereof are you made,
That millions of strange shadows on you tend?
Since every one hath, every one, one shade,
And you, but one, can every shadow lend.
Describe Adonis, and the counterfeit
Is poorly imated after you;
On Helen's cheek all art of beauty set,
And you in Grecian tires are painted new:
Speak of the spring and foison of the year;
The one doth shadow of your beauty show,
The other as your bounty doth appear;
And you in every blessed shape we know.
   In all external grace you have some part,
   But you like none, none you, for constant heart.

54

O, how much more doth beauty beauteous seem
By that sweet ornament which truth doth give!
The rose looks fair, but fairer we it deem
For that sweet odour which doth in it live.
The canker-blooms have full as deep a dye
As the perfumed tincture of the roses,
Hang on such thorns, and play as wantonly,
When summer's breath their masked buds discloses:
But, for their virtue only is their show,
They live unwoo'd, and unrespected fade;
Die to themselves. Sweet roses do not so;
Of their sweet deaths are sweetest odours made:
   And so of you, beauteous and lovely youth,
   When that shall vade, by verse distils your truth.

55

Not marble, nor the gilded monuments
Of princes, shall outlive this powerful rhyme;
But you shall shine more bright in these contents
Than unswept stone, besmear'd with sluttish time.
When wasteful war shall statues overturn,
And broils root out the work of masonry
Nor Mars his sword nor war's quick fire shall burn
The living record of your memory.
'Gainst death and all-oblivious enmity
Shall you pace forth; your praise shall still find room
Even in the eyes of all posterity
That wear this world out to the ending doom.
    So, till the judgement that yourself arise,
    You live in this, and dwell in lovers' eyes.

56

Sweet love, renew thy force; be it not said
Thy edge should blunter be than appetite,
Which but to-day by feeding is allay'd,
To-morrow sharpen'd in his former might:
So, love, be thou; although to-day thou fill
Thy hungry eyes even till they wink with fullness,
To-morrow see again, and do not kill
The spirit of love with a perpetual dullness.
Let this sad int'rim like the ocean be
Which parts the shore, where two contracted new
Come daily to the banks, that, when they see
Return of love, more blest may be the view;
    As call it winter, which, being full of care,
    Makes summer's welcome, thrice more wished, more rare.

57

Being your slave, what should I do but tend
Upon the hours and times of your desire?
I have no precious time at all to spend,
Nor services to do, till you require.
Nor dare I chide the world-without-end hour
Whilst I, my sovereign, watch the clock for you,
Nor think the bitterness of absence sour
When you have bid your servant once adieu;
Nor dare I question with my jealous thought
Where you may be, or your affairs suppose,
But, like a sad slave, stay and think of nought
Save, where you are how happy you make those.
    So true a fool is love, that in your will,
    Though you do any thing, he thinks no ill.

58

That god forbid that made me first your slave,
I should in thought control your times of pleasure,
Or at your hand the account of hours to crave,
Being your vassal, bound to stay your leisure!
O, let me suffer, being at your beck,
The imprison'd absence of your liberty;
And patience, tame to sufferance, bide each check,
Without accusing you of injury.
Be where you list, your charter is so strong,
That you yourself may privilege your time
To what you will; to you it doth belong
Yourself to pardon of self-doing crime.
    I am to wait, though waiting so be hell;
    Not blame your pleasure, be it ill or well.

59

If there be nothing new, but that which is
Hath been before, how are our brains beguiled,
Which, labouring for invention, bear amiss
The second burden of a former child!
O, that record could with a backward look,
Even of five hundred courses of the sun,
Show me your image in some antique book,
Since mind at first in character was done!
That I might see what the old world could say
To this composed wonder of your frame;
Whether we are mended, or where better they,
Or whether revolution be the same.
　　O, sure I am, the wits of former days
　　To subjects worse have given admiring praise.

60

Like as the waves make towards the pebbled shore,
So do our minutes hasten to their end;
Each changing place with that which goes before,
In sequent toil all forwards do contend.
Nativity, once in the main of light,
Crawls to maturity, wherewith being crown'd,
Crooked eclipses 'gainst his glory fight,
And Time that gave doth now his gift confound.
Time doth transfix the flourish set on youth,
And delves the parallels in beauty's brow;
Feeds on the rarities of nature's truth,
And nothing stands but for his scythe to mow:
　　And yet, to times in hope my verse shall stand,
　　Praising thy worth, despite his cruel hand.

61

Is it thy will thy image should keep open
My heavy eyelids to the weary night?
Dost thou desire my slumbers should be broken,
While shadows like to thee do mock my sight?
Is it thy spirit that thou send'st from thee
So far from home into my deeds to pry
To find out shames and idle hours in me,
The scope and tenour of thy jealousy?
O, no! thy love, though much, is not so great:
It is my love that keeps mine eye awake;
Mine own true love that doth my rest defeat,
To play the watchman ever for thy sake:
　　For thee watch I whilst thou dost wake elsewhere,
　　From me far off, with others all too near.

62

Sin of self-love possesseth all mine eye,
And all my soul, and all my every part;
And for this sin there is no remedy,
It is so grounded inward in my heart.
Methinks no face so gracious is as mine,
No shape so true, no truth of such account;
And for myself mine own worth do define,
As I all other in all worths surmount.
But when my glass shows me myself indeed,
Beated and chopped with tanned antiquity,
Mine own self-love quite contrary I read;
Self so self-loving were iniquity.
    'Tis thee, myself, that for myself I praise,
    Painting my age with beauty of thy days.

63

Against my love shall be, as I am now,
With Time's injurious hand crushed and o'erworn;
When hours have drain'd his blood, and fill'd his brow
With lines and wrinkles; when his youthful morn
Hath travell'd on to age's steepy night;
And all those beauties whereof now he's king
Are vanishing or vanished out of sight,
Stealing away the treasure of his spring;
For such a time do I now fortify
Against confounding age's cruel knife,
That he shall never cut from memory
My sweet love's beauty, though my lover's life:
    His beauty shall in these black lines be seen,
    And they shall live, and he in them still green.

64

When I have seen by Time's fell hand defaced
The rich proud cost of outworn buried age;
When sometime lofty towers I see down-razed,
And brass eternal slave to mortal rage;
When I have seen the hungry ocean gain
Advantage on the kingdom of the shore,
And the firm soil win of the watery main,
Increasing store with loss, and loss with store;
When I have seen such interchange of state,
Or state itself confounded to decay;
Ruin hath taught me thus to ruminate,–
That Time will come and take my love away.
    This thought is as a death, which cannot choose
    But weep to have that which it fears to lose.

65

Since brass, nor stone, nor earth, nor boundless sea,
But sad mortality o'ersways their power,
How with this rage shall beauty hold a plea,
Whose action is no stronger than a flower?
O, how shall summer's honey breath hold out
Against the wrackful siege of battering days,
When rocks impregnable are not so stout,
Nor gates of steel so strong, but Time decays?
O fearful meditation! where, alack,
Shall Time's best jewel from Time's chest lie hid?
Or what strong hand can hold his swift foot back,
Or who his spoil or beauty can forbid?
    O, none, unless this miracle have might,
    That in black ink my love may still shine bright.

66

Tired with all these, for restful death I cry,–
As, to behold Desert a beggar born,
And needy Nothing trimm'd in jollity,
And purest Faith unhappily forsworn,
And gilded Honour shamefully misplaced,
And maiden Virtue rudely strumpeted,
And right Perfection wrongfully disgraced,
And Strength by limping Sway disabled,
And Art made tongue-tied by Authority,
And Folly, doctor-like, controlling Skill,
And simple Truth miscall'd Simplicity,
And captive Good attending captain Ill:
    Tired with all these, from these would I be gone,
    Save that, to die, I leave my love alone.

67

Ah, wherefore with infection should he live,
And with his presence grace impiety,
That sin by him advantage should achieve,
And lace itself with his society?
Why should false painting imitate his cheek,
And steal dead seeing of his living hue?
Why should poor beauty indirectly seek
Roses of shadow, since his rose is true?
Why should he live, now Nature bankrout is,
Beggar'd of blood to blush through lively veins?
For she hath no exchequer now but his,
And, proud of many, lives upon his gains.
    O, him she stores, to show what wealth she had
    In days long since, before these last so bad.

68

Thus is his cheek the map of days outworn,
When beauty lived and died as flowers do now,
Before these bastard signs of fair were borne,
Or durst inhabit on a living brow;
Before the golden tresses of the dead,
The right of sepulchres, were shorn away,
To live a second life on second head;
Ere beauty's dead fleece made another gay:
In him those holy antique hours are seen,
Without all ornament, itself, and true,
Making no summer of another's green,
Robbing no old to dress his beauty new;
    And him as for a map doth Nature store,
    To show false Art what beauty was of yore.

69

Those parts of thee that the world's eye doth view
Want nothing that the thought of hearts can mend;
All tongues, the voice of souls, give thee that due,
Uttering bare truth, even so as foes commend.
Thy outward thus with outward praise is crown'd;
But those same tongues that give thee so thine own,
In other accents do this praise confound
By seeing farther than the eye hath shown.
They look into the beauty of thy mind,
And that, in guess, they measure by thy deeds;
Then churls, their thoughts, although their eyes were kind,
To thy fair flower add the rank smell of weeds:
　　But why thy odour matcheth not thy show,
　　The soil is this, that thou dost common grow.

70

That thou art blamed shall not be thy defect,
For slander's mark was ever yet the fair;
The ornament of beauty is suspect,
A crow that flies in heaven's sweetest air.
So thou be good, slander doth but approve
Thy worth the greater, being woo'd of time;
For canker vice the sweetest buds doth love,
And thou present'st a pure unstained prime.
Thou hast passed by the ambush of young days,
Either not assail'd, or victor being charged;
Yet this thy praise cannot be so thy praise,
To tie up envy evermore enlarged:
　　If some suspect of ill masked not thy show,
　　Then thou alone kingdoms of hearts shouldst owe.

71

No longer mourn for me when I am dead
Than you shall hear the surly sullen bell
Give warning to the world that I am fled
From this vile world, with vilest worms to dwell:
Nay, if you read this line, remember not
The hand that writ it; for I love you so,
That I in your sweet thoughts would be forgot,
If thinking on me then should make you woe.
O if, I say you look upon this verse
When I perhaps compounded am with clay,
Do not so much as my poor name rehearse;
But let your love even with my life decay;
　　Lest the wise world should look into your moan,
　　And mock you with me after I am gone.

72

O, lest the world should task you to recite
What merit lived in me, that you should love,
After my death, dear love, forget me quite,
For you in me can nothing worthy prove;
Unless you would devise some virtuous lie,
To do more for me than mine own desert,
And hang more praise upon deceased I
Than niggard truth would willingly impart:
O, lest your true love may seem false in this,
That you for love speak well of me untrue,
My name be buried where my body is,
And live no more to shame nor me nor you.
　　For I am shamed by that which I bring forth,
　　And so should you, to love things nothing worth.

73

That time of year thou mayst in me behold
When yellow leaves, or none, or few, do hang
Upon those boughs which shake against the cold,
Bare ruin'd choirs, where late the sweet birds sang.
In me thou see'st the twilight of such day
As after sunset fadeth in the west;
Which by and by black night doth take away,
Death's seccond self, that seals up all in rest.
In me thou see'st the glowing of such fire,
That on the ashes of his youth doth lie,
As the death-bed whereon it must expire,
Consumed with that which it was nourished by.
    This thou perceivest, which makes thy love more strong,
    To love that well which thou must leave ere long.

74

But be contented: when that fell arrest
Without all bail shall carry me away,
My life in this line some interest,
Which for memorial still with thee shall stay.
When thou reviewest this, thou dost review
The very part was consecrate to thee:
The earth can have but earth, which is his due;
My spirit is thine, the better part of me:
So, then, thou hast but lost the dregs of life,
The prey of worms, my body being dead;
The coward conquest of a wretch's knife,
Too base of thee to be remembered.
    The worth of that is that which it contains,
    And that is this, and this with thee remains.

75

So are you to my thoughts as food to life,
Or as sweet-season'd showers are to the ground;
And for the peace of you I hold such strife
As 'twixt a miser and his wealth is found;
Now proud as an enjoyer, and anon
Doubting the filching age will steal his treasure;
Now counting best to be with you alone,
Then better'd that the world may see my pleasure:
Sometime all full with feasting on your sight,
And by and by clean starved for a look;
Possessing or pursuing no delight,
Save what is had or must from you be took.
    Thus do I pine and surfeit day by day,
    Or gluttoning on all, or all away.

76

Why is my verse so barren of new pride,
So far from variation or quick change?
Why, with the time, do I not glance aside
To new-found methods and to compounds strange?
Why write I still all one, ever the same,
And keep invention in a noted weed,
That every word doth almost tell my name,
Showing their birth, and where they did proceed?
O, know, sweet love, I always write of you,
And you and love are still my argument;
So all my best is dressing old words new,
Spending again what is already spent:
    For as the sun is daily new and old,
    So is my love still telling what is told.

77

Thy glass will show thee how thy beauties wear,
Thy dial how thy precious minutes waste;
The vacant leaves thy mind's imprint will bear,
And of this book this learning mayst thou taste.
The wrinkles which thy glass will truly show,
Of mouthed graves will give thee memory;
Thou by thy dial's shady stealth mayst know
Time's thievish progress to eternity.
Look, what thy memory cannot contain,
Commit to these waste blanks, and thou shalt find
Those children nursed, deliver'd from thy brain
To take a new acquaintance of thy mind.
    These offices, so oft as thou wilt look,
    Shall profit thee, and much enrich thy book.

78

So oft have I invoked thee for my Muse,
And found such fair assistance in my verse,
As every alien pen hath got my use,
And under thee their poesy disperse.
Thine eyes, that taught the dumb on high to sing,
And heavy ignorance aloft to fly,
Have added feathers to the learned's wing,
And given grace a double majesty.
Yet be most proud of that which I compile,
Whose influence is thine, and born of thee:
In others' works thou dost but mend the style,
And arts with thy sweet graces graced be;
    But thou art all my art, and dost advance
    As high as learning my rude ignorance.

79

Whilst I alone did call upon thy aid,
My verse alone had all thy gentle grace;
But now my gracious numbers are decay'd,
And my sick Muse doth give another place.
I grant, sweet love, thy lovely argument
Deserves the travail of a worthier pen;
Yet what of thee thy poet doth invent
He robs thee of, and pays it thee again.
He lends thee virtue, and he stole that word
From thy behaviour; beauty doth he give,
And found it in thy cheek; he can afford
No praise to thee but what in thee doth live.
    Then thank him not for that which he doth say,
    Since what he owes thee thou thyself dost pay.

81

Or I shall live your epitaph to make,

Or you survive when I in earth am rotten;

From hence your memory death cannot take,

Although in me each part will be forgotten.

Your name from hence immortal life shall have,

Though I, once gone, to all the world must die:

The earth can yield me but a common grave,

When you entombed in men's eyes shall lie.

Your monument shall be my gentle verse,

Which eyes not yet created shall o'er-read;

And tongues to be your being shall rehearse,

When all the breathers of this world are dead;

    You still shall live—such virtue hath my pen—

    Where breath most breathes, ev'n in the mouths of men.

80

O, how I faint when I of you do write,

Knowing a better spirit doth use your name,

And in the praise thereof spends all his might,

To make me tongue-tied, speaking of your fame!

But since your worth, wide as the ocean is,

The humble as the proudest sail doth bear,

My saucy bark, inferior far to his,

On your broad main doth wilfully appear.

Your shallowest help will hold me up afloat,

While he upon your soundless deep doth ride;

Or, being wracked, I am a worthless boat,

He of tall building and of goodly pride:

    Then if he thrive, and I be cast away

    The worst was this; my love was my decay.

82

I grant thou wert not married to my Muse,

And therefore mayst without attaint o'erlook

The dedicated words which writers use

Of their fair subject, blessing every book.

Thou art as fair in knowledge as in hue,

Finding thy worth a limit past my praise;

And therefore art enforced to seek anew

Some fresher stamp of the time-bettering days.

And do so, love; yet when they have devised

What strained touches rhetoric can lend,

Thou truly fair wert truly sympathized

In true plain words by thy true-telling friend;

    And their gross painting might be better used,

    Where cheeks need blood; in thee it is abused.

83

I never saw that you did painting need,
And therefore to your fair no painting set;
I found, or thought I found, you did exceed
The barren tender of a poet's debt:
And therefore have I slept in your report,
That you yourself, being extant, well might show
How far a modern quill doth come too short,
Speaking of worth, what worth in you doth grow.
This silence for my sin you did impute,
Which shall be most my glory, being dumb;
For I impair not beauty, being mute,
When others would give life, and bring a tomb.
    There lives more life in one of your fair eyes
    Than both your poets can in praise devise.

84

Who is it that says most? which can say more
Than this rich praise, that you alone are you?
In whose confine immured is the store
Which should example where your equal grew.
Lean penury within that pen doth dwell
That to his subject lends not some small glory;
But he that writes of you, if he can tell
That you are you, so dignifies his story:
Let him but copy what in you is writ,
Not making worse what nature made so clear,
And such a counterpart shall fame his wit,
Making his style admired everywhere.
    You to your beauteous blessings add a curse,
    Being fond on praise, which makes your praises worse.

85

My tongue-tied Muse in manners holds her still,
While comments of your praise, richly compiled,
Reserve their character with golden quill,
And precious phrase by all the Muses filed.
I think good thoughts, whilst other write good words,
And, like unletter'd clerk, still cry Amen
To every hymn that able spirit affords
In polished form of well-refined pen.
Hearing you praised, I say 'Tis so, 'tis true,'
And to the most of praise add something more;
But that is in my thought, whose love to you,
Though words come hindmost, holds his rank before.
    Then others for the breath of words respect,
    Me for my dumb thoughts, speaking in effect.

86

Was it the proud full sail of his great verse,
Bound for the prize of all-too-precious you,
That did my ripe thoughts in my brain inhearse,
Making their tomb the womb wherein they grew?
Was it his spirit, by spirits taught to write
Above a mortal pitch, that struck me dead?
No, neither he, nor his compeers by night
Giving him aid, my verse astonished.
He, nor that affable familiar ghost
Which nightly gulls him with intelligence,
As victors, of my silence cannot boast;
I was not sick of any fear from thence:
    But when your countenance fill'd up his line,
    Then lacked I matter; that enfeebled mine.

87

Farewell! thou art too dear for my possessing,
And like enough thou know'st thy estimate:
The charter of thy worth gives thee releasing;
My bonds in thee are all determinate.
For how do I hold thee but by thy granting?
And for that riches where is my deserving?
The cause of this fair gift in me is wanting,
And so my patent back again is swerving.
Thyself thou gavest, thy own worth then not knowing,
Or me, to whom thou gavest it, else mistaking;
So thy great gift, upon misprision growing,
Comes home again, on better judgement making.
    Thus have I had thee, as a dream doth flatter,
    In sleep a king, but waking no such matter.

88

When thou shalt be disposed to set me light,
And place my merit in the eye of scorn,
Upon thy side against myself I'll fight,
And prove thee virtuous, though thou art forsworn.
With mine own weakness being best acquainted,
Upon thy part I can set down a story
Of faults conceal'd, wherein I am attainted;
That thou, in losing me, shall win much glory:
And I by this will be a gainer too;
For bending all my loving thoughts on thee,
The injuries that to myself I do,
Doing thee vantage, double-vantage me.
    Such is my love, to thee I so belong,
    That for thy right myself will bear all wrong.

89

Say that thou didst forsake me for some fault,
And I will comment upon that offence:
Speak of my lameness, and I straight will halt,
Against thy reasons making no defence.
Thou canst not, love, disgrace me half so ill,
To set a form upon desired change,
As I'll myself disgrace: knowing thy will,
I will acquaintance strangle, and look strange;
Be absent from thy walks; and in my tongue
Thy sweet beloved name no more shall dwell,
Lest I, too much profane, should do it wrong,
And haply of our old acquaintance tell.
    For thee, against myself I'll vow debate,
    For I must ne'er love him whom thou dost hate.

90

Then hate me when thou wilt; if ever, now;
Now, while the world is bent my deeds to cross,
Join with the spite of fortune, make me bow,
And do not drop in for an after-loss:
Ah, do not, when my heart hath 'scaped this sorrow,
Come in the rearward of a conquer'd woe;
Give not a windy night a rainy morrow,
To linger out a purposed overthrow.
If thou wilt leave me, do not leave me last,
When other petty griefs have done their spite,
But in the onset come: so shall I taste
At first the very worst of fortune's might;
    And other strains of woe, which now seem woe,
    Compared with loss of thee will not seem so.

92

But do thy worst to steal thyself away,
For term of life thou art assured mine;
And life no longer than thy love will stay,
For it depends upon that love of thine.
Then need I not to fear the worst of wrongs,
When in the least of them my life hath end.
I see a better state to me belongs
Than that which on thy humour doth depend:
Thou canst not vex me with inconstant mind,
Since that my life on thy revolt doth lie.
O, what a happy title do I find,
Happy to have thy love, happy to die!
  But what's so blessed-fair that fears no blot?
  Thou mayst be false, and yet I know it not.

91

Some glory in their birth, some in their skill,
Some in their wealth, some in their body's force;
Some in their garments, though new-fangled ill;
Some in their hawks and hounds, some in their horse;
And every humour hath his adjunct pleasure,
Wherein it finds a joy above the rest:
But these particulars are not my measure;
All these I better in one general best.
Thy love is better than high birth to me,
Richer than wealth, prouder than garments' cost,
Of more delight than hawks or horses be;
And having thee, of all men's pride I boast:
  Wretched in this alone, that thou mayst take
  All this away, and me most wretched make.

93

So shall I live, supposing thou art true,
Like a deceived husband; so love's face
May still seem love to me, though alter'd new;
Thy looks with me, thy heart in other place:
For there can live no hatred in thine eye,
Therefore in that I cannot know thy change.
In many's looks the false heart's history
Is writ in moods and frowns and wrinkles strange;
But heaven in thy creation did decree
That in thy face sweet love should ever dwell;
Whate'er thy thoughts or thy heart's workings be,
Thy looks should nothing thence but sweetness tell.
  How like Eve's apple doth thy beauty grow,
  If thy sweet virtue answer not thy show!

94

They that have power to hurt and will do none,
That do not do the thing they most do show,
Who, moving others, are themselves as stone,
Unmoved, cold, and to temptation slow;
They rightly do inherit heaven's graces,
And husband nature's riches from expense;
They are the lords and owners of their faces,
Others but stewards of their excellence.
The summer's flower is to the summer sweet,
Though to itself it only live and die;
But if that flower with base infection meet,
The basest weed outbraves his dignity:
　　For sweetest things turn sourest by their deeds;
　　Lilies that fester smell far worse than weeds.

95

How sweet and lovely dost thou make the shame
Which, like a canker in the fragrant rose,
Doth spot the beauty of thy budding name!
O, in what sweets dost thou thy sins enclose!
That tongue that tells the story of thy days,
Making lascivious comments on thy sport,
Cannot dispraise but in a kind of praise;
Naming thy name blesses an ill report.
O, what a mansion have those vices got
Which for their habitation chose out thee,
Where beauty's veil doth cover every blot,
And all things turns to fair that eyes can see!
　　Take heed, dear heart, of this large privilege;
　　The hardest knife ill-used doth lose his edge.

96

Some say, thy fault is youth, some wantonness;
Some say, thy grace is youth and gentle sport;
Both grace and faults are loved of more and less:
Thou mak'st faults graces that to thee resort.
As on the finger of a throned queen
The basest jewel will be well esteem'd,
So are those errors that in thee are seen
To truths translated, and for true things deem'd.
How many lambs might the stern wolf betray,
If like a lamb he could his looks translate!
How many gazers mightst thou lead away,
If thou wouldst use the strength of all thy state!
　　But do not so, I love thee in such sort
　　As thou being mine, mine is thy good report.

97

How like a winter hath my absence been
From thee, the pleasure of the fleeting year!
What freezings have I felt, what dark days seen!
What old December's bareness everywhere!
And yet this time removed was summer's time;
The teeming autumn, big with rich increase,
Bearing the wanton burden of the prime,
Like widowed wombs after their lords' decease:
Yet this abundant issue seem'd to me
But hope of orphans and unfather'd fruit;
For summer and his pleasures wait on thee,
And, thou away, the very birds are mute;
 Or, if they sing, 'tis with so dull a cheer,
 That leaves look pale, dreading the winter's near.

98

From you have I been absent in the spring,
When proud-pied April, dressed in all his trim,
Hath put a spirit of youth in everything,
That heavy Saturn laughed and leapt with him.
Yet nor the lays of birds, nor the sweet smell
Of different flowers in odour and in hue,
Could make me any summer's story tell,
Or from their proud lap pluck them where they grew:
Nor did I wonder at the lily's white,
Nor praise the deep vermilion in the rose;
They were but sweet, but figures of delight,
Drawn after you, you pattern of all those.
 Yet seem'd it winter still, and, you away,
 As with your shadow I with these did play.

99

The forward violet thus did I chide:
Sweet thief, whence didst thou steal thy sweet that smells,
If not from my love's breath? The purple pride
Which on thy soft cheek for complexion dwells
In my love's veins thou hast too grossly dyed.
The lily I condemned for thy hand;
And buds of marjoram had stol'n thy hair:
The roses fearfully on thorns did stand,
One blushing shame, another white despair;
A third, nor red nor white, had stol'n of both,
And to his robbery had annexed thy breath;
But, for his theft, in pride of all his growth
A vengeful canker ate him up to death.
 More flowers I noted, yet I none could see
 But sweet or colour it had stol'n from thee.

100

Where art thou, Muse; that thou forgett'st so long
To speak of that which gives thee all thy might?
Spend'st thou thy fury on some worthless song,
Dark'ning thy power to lend base subjects light?
Return, forgetful Muse, and straight redeem
In gentle numbers time idly spent
Sing to the ear that doth thy lays esteem;
And gives thy pen both skill and argument.
Rise, resty Muse, my love's sweet face survey,
If Time have any wrinkle graven there;
If any, be a satire to decay,
And make Time's spoils despised everywhere.
 Give my love fame faster than Time wastes life;
 So thou prevent'st his scythe and crooked knife.

101

O truant Muse, what shall be thy amends
For thy neglect of truth in beauty dyed?
Both truth and beauty on my love depends,
So dost thou too, and therein dignified.
Make answer, Muse, wilt thou not haply say,
Truth needs no colour, with his colour fixed,
Beauty no pencil, beauty's truth to lay,
But best is best, if never intermixed?
Because he needs no praise, wilt thou be dumb?
Excuse not silence so: for't lies in thee
To make him much outlive a gilded tomb,
And to be praised of ages yet to be.
   Then do thy office, Muse, I teach thee how
   To make him seem long hence as he shows now.

102

My love is strengthen'd though more weak in seeming;
I love not less, though less the show appear:
That love is merchandized whose rich esteeming
The owner's tongue doth publish everywhere.
Our love was new, and then but in the spring,
When I was wont to greet it with my lays;
As Philomel in summer's front doth sing,
And stops her pipe in growth of riper days:
Not that the summer is less pleasant now
Than when her mournful hymns did hush the night,
But that wild music burdens every bough,
And sweets grown common lose their dear delight.
   Therefore, like her, I sometime hold my tongue,
   Because I would not dull you with my song.

103

Alack, what poverty my Muse brings forth,
That having such a scope to show her pride,
The argument, all bare, is of more worth
Than when it hath my added praise beside!
O, blame me not, if I no more can write!
Look in your glass, and there appears a face
That overgoes my blunt invention quite,
Dulling my lines, and doing me disgrace.
Were it not sinful, then, striving to mend,
To mar the subject that before was well?
For to no other pass my verses tend
Than of your graces and your gifts to tell;
   And more, much more, than in my verse can sit,
   Your own glass shows you when you look in it.

104

To me, fair friend, you never can be old,
For as you were when first your eye I eyed,
Such seems your beauty still. Three winters' cold
Have from the forests shook three summers' pride;
Three beauteous springs to yellow autumn turn'd
In process of the seasons have I seen,
Three April perfumes in three hot Junes burn'd,
Since first I saw you fresh, which yet are green.
Ah, yet doth beauty, like a dial-hand,
Steal from his figure, and no pace perceived;
So your sweet hue, which methinks still doth stand,
Hath motion, and mine eye may be deceived:
   For fear of which, hear this, thou age unbred,—
   Ere you were born was beauty's summer dead.

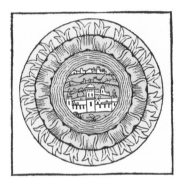

106

When in the chronicle of wasted time
I see descriptions of the fairest wights,
And beauty making beautiful old rhyme
In praise of ladies dead and lovely knights,
Then, in the blazon of sweet beauty's best,
Of hand, of foot, of lip, of eye, of brow,
I see their antique pen would have expressed
Even such a beauty as you master now.
So all their praises are but prophecies
Of this our time, all you prefiguring;
And, for they looked but with divining eyes,
They had not skill enough your worth to sing:
    For we, which now behold these present days,
    Have eyes to wonder, but lack tongues to praise.

105

Let not my love be call'd idolatry,
Nor my beloved as an idol show,
Since all alike my songs and praises be
To one, of one, still such, and ever so.
Kind is my love to-day, to-morrow kind
Still constant in a wondrous excellence;
Therefore my verse to constancy confined,
One thing expressing, leaves out difference.
Fair, kind, and true, is all my argument,—
Fair, kind, and true, varying to other words;
And in this change is my invention spent,
Three themes in one, which wondrous scope affords.
    Fair, kind, and true, have often lived alone,
    Which three till now never kept seat in one.

107

Not mine own fears, nor the prophetic soul
Of the wide world dreaming on things to come,
Can yet the lease of my true love control,
Supposed as forfeit to a confined doom.
The mortal moon hath her eclipse endured,
And the sad augurs mock their own presage;
Incertainties now crown themselves assured,
And peace proclaims olives of endless age.
Now with the drops of this most balmy time
My love looks fresh, and Death to me subscribes,
Since, spite of him, I'll live in this poor rhyme,
While he insults o'er dull and speechless tribes:
    And thou in this shalt find thy monument,
    When tyrants' crests and tombs of brass are spent.

108

What's in the brain, that ink may character,
Which hath not figured to thee my true spirit?
What's new to speak, what new to register,
That may express my love, or thy dear merit?
Nothing, sweet boy; but yet, like prayers divine,
I must each day say o'er the very same;
Counting no old thing old, thou mine, I thine,
Even as when first I hallow'd thy fair name,
So that eternal love in love's fresh case
Weighs not the dust and injury of age,
Nor gives to necessary wrinkles place,
But makes antiquity for aye his page;
    Finding the first conceit of love there bred,
    Where time and outward form would show it dead.

109

O, never say that I was false of heart,
Though absence seem'd my flame to qualify.
As easy might I from myself depart
As from my soul, which in thy breast doth lie:
That is my home of love: if I have ranged,
Like him that travels I return again,
Just to the time, not with the time exchanged,
So that myself bring water for my stain.
Never believe, though in my nature reign'd
All frailties that besiege all kinds of blood,
That it could so preposterously be stain'd,
To leave for nothing all thy sum of good;
    For nothing this wide universe I call,
    Save thou, my rose; in it thou art my all.

110

Alas, 'tis true I have gone here and there,
And made myself a motley to the view,
Gored mine own thoughts, sold cheap what is most dear,
Made old offences of affections new;
Most true it is, that I have looked on truth
Askance and strangely: but, by all above,
These blenches gave my heart another youth,
And worse essays proved thee my best of love.
Now all is done, have what shall have no end:
Mine appetite I never more will grind
On newer proof, to try an older friend,
A god in love, to whom I am confined.
    Then give me welcome, next my heaven the best,
    Even to thy pure and most most loving breast.

111

O, for my sake do you wish Fortune chide,
The guilty goddess of my harmful deeds,
That did not better for my life provide
Than public means which public manners breeds.
Thence comes it that my name receives a brand;
And almost thence my nature is subdued
To what it works in, like the dyer's hand:
Pity me, then, and wish I were renew'd;
Whilst, like a willing patient, I will drink
Potions of eisel 'gainst my strong infection;
No bitterness that I will bitter think,
Nor double penance, to correct correction.
    Pity me, then, dear friend, and I assure ye
    Even that your pity is enough to cure me.

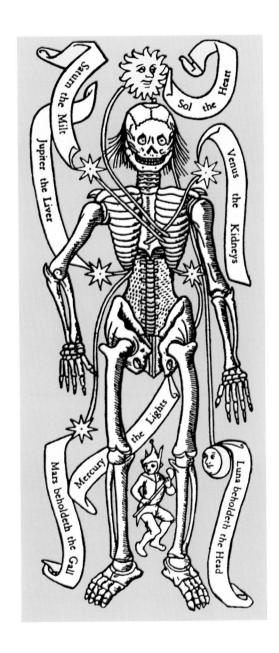

112

Your love and pity doth the impression fill
Which vulgar scandal stamped upon my brow;
For what care I who calls me well or ill,
So you o'er-green my bad, my good allow?
You are my all-the-world, and I must strive
To know my shames and praises from your tongue;
None else to me, nor I to none alive,
That my steel'd sense or changes right or wrong.
In so profound abysm I throw all care
Of others' voices, that my adder's sense
To critic and to flatterer stopped are.
Mark how with my neglect, I do dispense:
　　You are so strongly in my purpose bred,
　　That all the world besides me thinks y'are dead.

113

Since I left you, mine eye is in my mind;
And that which governs me to go about
Doth part his function, and is partly blind,
Seems seeing, but effectually is out;
For it no form delivers to the heart
Of bird, of flower, or shape, which it doth latch:
Of his quick objects hath the mind no part,
Nor his own vision holds what it doth catch;
For if it see the rudest or gentlest sight,
The most sweet favour or deformed'st creature,
The mountain, or the sea, the day, or night,
The crow, or dove, it shapes them to your feature:
　　Incapable of more, replete with you,
　　My most true mind thus maketh m'eyne untrue.

114

Or whether doth my mind, being crown'd with you,
Drink up the monarch's plague, this flattery?
Or whether shall I say, mine eye saith true,.
And that your love taught it this alchemy,
To make of monsters and things indigest
Such cherubins as your sweet self resemble,
Creating every bad a perfect best,
As fast as objects to his beams assemble?
O,'tis the first; 'tis flatt'ry in my seeing,
And my great mind most kingly drinks it up:
Mine eye well knows what with his gust is greeing,
And to his palate doth prepare the cup:
　　If it be poison'd, 'tis the lesser sin
　　That mine eye loves it, and doth first begin.

115

Those lines that I before have writ do lie,
Even those that said I could not love you dearer.
Yet then my judgement knew no reason why
My most full flame should afterwards burn clearer.
But reckoning Time, whose million'd accidents
Creep in 'twixt vows, and change decrees of kings,
Tan sacred beauty, blunt the sharp'st intents,
Divert strong minds to the course of alt'ring things;
Alas, why, fearing of Time's tyranny,
Might I not then say, now I love you best,
When I was certain o'er incertainty,
Crowning the present, doubting of the rest?
　　Love is a babe; then might I not say so,
　　To give full growth to that which still doth grow.

116

Let me not to the marriage of true minds
Admit impediments. Love is not love
Which alters when it alteration finds,
Or bends with the remover to remove:
O, no! it is an ever-fixed mark,
That looks on tempests, and is never shaken,
It is the star to every wandering bark,
Whose worth's unknown, although his height be taken.
Love's not Time's fool, though rosy lips and cheeks
Within his bending sickle's compass come;
Love alters not with his brief hours and weeks,
But bears it out even to the edge of doom.
　　If this be error, and upon me proved,
　　I never writ, nor no man ever loved.

117

Accuse me thus: that l have scanted all
Wherein I should your great deserts repay;
Forgot upon your dearest love to call,
Whereto all bonds do tie me day by day;
That I have frequent been with unknown minds,
And given to time your own dear-purchased right;
That I have hoisted sail to all the winds
Which should transport me farthest from your sight.
Book both my wilfulness and errors down,
And on just proof surmise accumulate;
Bring me within the level of your frown,
But shoot not at me in your waken'd hate;
　　Since my appeal says I did strive to prove
　　The constancy and virtue of your love.

118

Like as, to make our appetites more keen,
With eager compounds we our palate urge;
As, to prevent our maladies unseen,
We sicken to shun sickness when we purge;
Even so being full of your ne'er-cloying sweetness,
To bitter sauces did I frame my feeding;
And, sick of welfare, found a kind of meetness
To be diseased, ere that there was true needing.
Thus policy in love, t'anticipate
The ills that were not, grew to faults assured,
And brought to medicine a healthful state,
Which, rank of goodness, would by ill be cured:
　　But thence I learn, and find the lesson true,
　　Drugs poison him that so fell sick of you.

119

What potions have I drunk of Siren tears,
Distill'd from limbecks foul as hell within,
Applying fears to hopes, and hopes to fears,
Still losing when I saw myself to win!
What wretched errors hath my heart committed,
Whilst it hath thought itself so blessed never!
How have mine eyes out of their spheres been fitted
In the distraction of this madding fever!
O benefit of ill! now I find true
That better is by evil still made better;
And ruin'd love, when it is built anew,
Grows fairer than at first, more strong, far greater.
　　So I return rebuked to my content,
　　And gain by ills thrice more than I have spent.

120

That you were once unkind befriends me now,
And for that sorrow which I then did feel
Needs must I under my transgression bow,
Unless my nerves were brass or hammered steel.
For if you were by my unkindness shaken,
As I by yours, y'have past a hell of time;
And I, a tyrant, have no leisure taken
To weigh how once I suffer'd in your crime.
O, that our night of woe might have remember'd
My deepest sense, how hard true sorrow hits,
And soon to you, as you to me then, tender'd
The humble salve which wounded bosoms fits!
　　But that, your trespass, now becomes a fee;
　　Mine ransoms yours, and yours must ransom me.

121

'Tis better to be vile than vile esteemed,
When not to be receives reproach of being;
And the just pleasure lost, which is so deemed
Not by our feeling, but by others' seeing:
For why should others' false adulterate eyes
Give salutation to my sportive blood?
Or on my frailties why are frailer spies,
Which in their wills count bad what I think good?
No, I am that I am; and they that level
At my abuses reckon up their own:
I may be straight, though they themselves be bevel;
By their rank thoughts my deeds must not be shown;
　　Unless this general evil they maintain–
　　All men are bad, and in their badness reign.

122

Thy gift, thy tables, are within my brain
Full character'd with lasting memory,
Which shall above that idle rank remain,
Beyond all date, even to eternity:
Or, at the least, so long as brain and heart:
Have faculty by nature to subsist;
Till each to razed oblivion yield his part
Of thee, thy record never can be missed.
That poor retention could not so much hold,
Nor need I tallies thy dear love to score;
Therefore to give them from me was I bold,
To trust those tables that receive thee more:
　　To keep an adjunct to remember thee
　　Were to import forgetfulness in me.

THE THAMES AT GREAT MARLOW

123

No, Time, thou shalt not boast that I do change:
Thy pyramids built up with newer might
To me are nothing novel, nothing strange;
They are but dressings of a former sight.
Our dates are brief, and therefore we admire
What thou dost foist upon us that is old;
And rather make them born to our desire
Than think that we before have heard them told.
Thy registers and thee I both defy,
Not wondering at the present nor the past;
For thy records and what we see doth lie,
Made more or less by thy continual haste.
   This I do vow, and this shall ever be,
   I will be true, despite thy scythe and thee.

124

If my dear love were but the child of state,
It might for Fortune's bastard be unfather'd,
As subject to Time's love or to Time's hate,
Weeds among weeds, or flow'rs with flowers gathered.
No, it was builded far from accident;
It suffers not in smiling pomp, nor falls
Under the blow of thralled discontent,
Whereto the inviting time our fashion calls:
It fears not policy, that heretic,
Which works on leases of short-number'd hours,
But all alone stands hugely politic,
That it nor grows with heat nor drowns with showers.
   To this I witness call the fools of Time,
   Which die for goodness, who have lived for crime.

125

Were't ought to me I bore the canopy,
With my extern the outward honouring,
Or laid great bases for eternity,
Which proves more short than waste or ruining?
Have I not seen dwellers on form and favour
Lose all, and more, by paying too much rent,
For compound sweet foregoing simple savour,
Pitiful thrivers, in their gazing spent?
No, let me be obsequious in thy heart,
And take thou my oblation, poor but free,
Which is not mixed with seconds, knows no art,
But mutual render, only me for thee.
   Hence, thou suborn'd informer! a true soul
   When most impeached stands least in thy control.

126

O thou, my lovely boy, who in thy power
Dost hold Time's fickle glass, his sickle-hour;
Who hast by waning grown, and therein show'st
Thy lovers withering, as thy sweet self grow'st;
If Nature, sovereign mistress over wrack,
As thou goest onwards still will pluck thee back,
She keeps thee to this purpose, that her skill
May Time disgrace, and wretched minute kill.
Yet fear her, O thou minion of her pleasure!
She may detain, but not still keep, her treasure:
   Her audit, though delay'd, answer'd must be,
   And her quietus is to render thee.

127

In the old age black was not counted fair,
Or if it were, it bore not beauty's name;
But now is black beauty's successive heir,
And beauty slander'd with a bastard shame:
For since each hand hath put on nature's power,
Fairing the foul with art's false borrow'd face,
Sweet beauty hath no name, no holy bower,
But is profaned, if not lives in disgrace.
Therefore my mistress' eyes are raven black,
Her eyes so suited, and they mourners seem
At such who, not born fair, no beauty lack,
Slandering creation with a false esteem:
    Yet so they mourn, becoming of their woe,
    That every tongue says beauty should look so.

128

How oft, when thou, my music, music play'st,
Upon that blessed wood whose motion sounds
With thy sweet fingers, when thou gently sway'st
The wiry concord that mine ear confounds,
Do I envy those jacks that nimble leap
To kiss the tender inward of thy hand,
Whilst my poor lips, which should that harvest reap,
At the wood's boldness by thee blushing stand!
To be so tickled, they would change their state
And situation with those dancing chips,
O'er whom thy fingers walk with gentle gait,
Making dead wood more blest than living lips.
    Since saucy jacks so happy are in this,
    Give them thy fingers, me thy lips to kiss.

129

Th' expense of spirit in a waste of shame
Is lust in action; and till action, lust
Is perjured, murd'rous, bloody, full of blame,
Savage, extreme, rude, cruel, not to trust;
Enjoy'd no sooner but despised straight;
Past reason hunted; and no sooner had,
Past reason hated, as a swallow'd bait,
On purpose laid to make the taker mad:
Mad in pursuit, and in possession so;
Had, having, and in quest to have, extreme
A bliss in proof, and proved, a very woe;
Before, a joy proposed; behind, a dream.
    All this the world well knows; yet none knows well
    To shun the heaven that leads men to this hell.

131

Thou art as tyrannous, so as thou art,
As those whose beauties proudly make them cruel;
For well thou know'st to my dear doting heart
Thou art the fairest and most precious jewel.
Yet, in good faith, some say that thee behold,
Thy face hath not the power to make love groan.
To say they err I dare not be so bold,
Although I swear it to myself alone.
And, to be sure that is not false I swear,
A thousand groans, but thinking on thy face,
One on another's neck, do witness bear
Thy black is fairest in my judgement's place.
    In nothing art thou black save in thy deeds,
    And thence this slander, as I think, proceeds.

130

My mistress' eyes are nothing like the sun;
Coral is far more red than her lips' red:
If snow be white, why then her breasts are dun;
If hairs be wires, black wires grow on her head.
I have seen roses damasked, red and white,
But no such roses see I in her cheeks;
And in some perfumes is there more delight
Than in the breath that from my mistress reeks.
I love to hear her speak, yet well I know
That music hath a far more pleasing sound:
I grant I never saw a goddess go;
My mistress, when she walks, treads on the ground.
    And yet, by heaven, I think my love as rare
    As any she belied with false compare.

132

Thine eyes I love, and they, as pitying me,
Knowing thy heart torment me with disdain,
Have put on black, and loving mourners be,
Looking with pretty ruth upon my pain.
And truly not the morning sun of heaven
Better becomes the gray cheeks of the east,
Nor that full star that ushers in the even
Doth half that glory to the sober west,
As those two mourning eyes become thy face:
O, let it, then, as well beseem thy heart
To mourn for me, since mourning doth thee grace,
And suit thy pity like in every part.
    Then will I swear Beauty herself is black,
    And all they foul that thy complexion lack.

133

Beshrew that heart that makes my heart to groan
For that deep wound it gives my friend and me!
Is't not enough to torture me alone,
But slave to slavery my sweet'st friend must be?
Me from myself thy cruel eye hath taken,
And my next self thou harder hast engrossed:
Of him, myself, and thee, I am forsaken;
A torment thrice threefold thus to be crossed.
Prison my heart in thy steel bosom's ward,
But then my friend's heart let my poor heart bail;
Whoe'er keeps me, let my heart be his guard,
Thou canst not then use rigour in my jail:
    And yet thou wilt; for I, being pent in thee,
    Perforce am thine, and all that is in me.

134

So, now I have confessed that he is thine,
And I myself am mortgaged to thy will,
Myself I'll forfeit, so that other mine
Thou wilt restore, to be my comfort still:
But thou wilt not, nor he will not be free,
For thou art covetous, and he is kind;
He learn'd but, surety-like, to write for me,
Under that bond that him as fast doth bind.
The statute of thy beauty thou wilt take,
Thou usurer, that put'st forth all to use,
And sue a friend came debtor for my sake;
So him I lose through my unkind abuse.
    Him have I lost; thou hast both him and me:
    He pays the whole, and yet am I not free.

135

Whoever hath her wish, thou hast thy Will,
And Will to boot, and Will in overplus;
More than enough am I that vex thee still,
To thy sweet will making addition thus.
Wilt thou, whose will is large and spacious,
Not once vouchsafe to hide my will in thine?
Shall will in others seem right gracious,
And in my will no fair acceptance shine?
The sea, all water, yet receives rain still,
And in abundance addeth to his store;
So thou, being rich in Will, add to thy Will
One will of mine, to make thy large Will more.
    Let no unkind, no fair beseechers kill;
    Think all but one, and me in that one Will.

136

If thy soul check thee that I come so near,
Swear to thy blind soul that I was thy Will,
And will, thy soul knows, is admitted there;
Thus far for love my love-suit, sweet, fulfil.
Will will fulfil the treasure of thy love,
Ay, fill it full with wills, and my will one.
In things of great receipt with ease we prove
Among a number one is reckon'd none:
Then in the number let me pass untold,
Though in thy store's account I one must be;
For nothing hold me, so it please thee hold
That nothing me; a something, sweet, to thee:
    Make but my name thy love, and love that still,
    And then thou lov'st me for my name is Will.

137

Thou blind fool, love, what dost thou to mine eyes,
That they behold, and see not what they see?
They know what beauty is, see where it lies,
Yet what the best is take the worst to be.
If eyes, corrupt by over-partial looks,
Be anchor'd in the bay where all men ride;
Why of eyes' falsehood hast thou forged hooks,
Whereto the judgement of my heart is tied?
Why should my heart think that a several plot
Which my heart knows the wide world's common place?
Or mine eyes seeing this, say this is not,
To put fair truth upon so foul a face?
 In things right-true my heart and eyes have erred,
 And to this false plague are they now transferred.

138

When my love swears that she is made of truth,
I do believe her, though I know she lies,
That she might think me some untutor'd youth,
Unlearned in the world's false subtleties.
Thus vainly thinking that she thinks me young,
Although she knows my days are past the best,
Simply I credit her false-speaking tongue:
On both sides thus is simple truth suppressed.
But wherefore says she not she is unjust?
And wherefore say not I that I am old?
O, love's best habit is in seeming trust,
And age in love loves not to have years told:
 Therefore I lie with her and she with me,
 And in our faults by lies, we flatter'd be.

139

O, call not me to justify the wrong
That thy unkindness lays upon my heart;
Wound me not with thine eye, but with thy tongue
Use power with power, and slay me not by art.
Tell me thou lovest elsewhere; but in my sight,
Dear heart, forbear to glance thine eye aside:
What need'st thou wound with cunning, when thy might
Is more than my o'erpressed defence can bide?
Let me excuse thee: ah, my love well knows
Her pretty looks have been mine enemies;
And therefore from my face she turns my foes,
That they elsewhere might dart their injuries:
 Yet do not so; but since I am near slain,
 Kill me outright with looks, and rid my pain.

140

Be wise as thou art cruel; do not press
My tongue-tied patience with too much disdain;
Lest sorrow lend me words, and words express
The manner of my pity-wanting pain.
If I might teach thee wit, better it were,
Though not to love, yet, love, to tell me so;
As testy sick men, when their deaths be near,
No news but health from their physicians know;
For, if I should despair, I should grow mad,
And in my madness might speak ill of thee:
Now this ill-wresting world is grown so bad,
Mad slanderers by mad ears believed be.
 That I may not be so, nor thou belied,
 Bear thine eyes straight, though thy proud heart go wide.

141

In faith, I do not love thee with mine eyes,
For they in thee a thousand errors note;
But 'tis my heart that loves what they despise,
Who, in despite of view, is pleased to dote;
Nor are mine ears with thy tongue's tune delighted;
Nor tender feeling to base touches prone,
Nor taste, nor smell, desire to be invited
To any sensual feast with thee alone:
But my five wits nor my five senses can
Dissuade one foolish heart from serving thee,
Who leaves unsway'd the likeness of a man,
Thy proud heart's slave and vassal wretch to be:
    Only my plague thus far I count my gain,
    That she that makes me sin awards me pain.

142

Love is my sin, and thy dear virtue hate,
Hate of my sin, grounded on sinful loving:
O, but with mine compare thou thine own state,
And thou shalt find it merits not reproving;
Or, if it do, not from those lips of thine,
That have profaned their scarlet ornaments
And seal'd false bonds of love as oft as mine,
Robb'd others' beds' revenues of their rents.
Be it lawful I love thee, as thou lovest those
Whom thine eyes woo as mine importune thee:
Root pity in thy heart, that, when it grows,
Thy pity may deserve to pitied be.
    If thou dost seek to have what thou dost hide,
    By self-example mayst thou be denied!

143

Lo, as a careful housewife runs to catch
One of her feather'd creatures broke away,
Sets down her babe, and makes all swift dispatch
In pursuit of the thing she would have stay;
Whilst her neglected child holds her in chase,
Cries to catch her whose busy care is bent
To follow that which flies before her face,
Not prizing her poor infant's discontent:
So run'st thou after that which flies from thee,
Whilst I thy babe chase thee afar behind;
But if thou catch thy hope, turn back to me,
And play the mother's part, kiss me, be kind:
    So will I pray that thou mayst have thy Will,
    If thou turn back, and my loud crying still.

144

Two loves I have of comfort and despair,
Which like two spirits do suggest me still:
The better angel is a man right fair,
The worser spirit a woman colour'd ill.
To win me soon to hell, my female evil
Tempteth my better angel from my side,
And would corrupt my saint to be a devil,
Wooing his purity with her foul pride
And whether that my angel be turn'd fiend,
Suspect I may, yet not directly tell;
But being both from me, both to each friend,
I guess one angel in another's hell:
    Yet this shall I ne'er know, but live in doubt,
    Till my bad angel fire my good one out.

145

Those lips that Love's own hand did make
Breathed forth the sound that said 'I hate'
To me that languished for her sake:
But when she saw my woeful state,
Straight in her heart did mercy come,
Chiding that tongue that ever sweet
Was used in giving gentle doom;
And taught it thus anew to greet;
'I hate' she alter'd with an end,
That follow'd it as gentle day
Doth follow night, who like a fiend
From heaven to hell is flown away;
   'I hate' from hate away she threw,
    And saved my life, saying– 'Not you.'

146

Poor soul, the centre of my sinful earth–
My sinful earth these rebel powers that thee array–
Why dost thou pine within and suffer dearth,
Painting thy outward walls so costly gay?
Why so large cost, having so short a lease,
Dost thou upon thy fading mansion spend?
Shall worms, inheritors of this excess,
Eat up thy charge? Is this thy body's end?
Then, soul, live thou upon thy servant's loss,
And let that pine to aggravate thy store;
Buy terms divine in selling hours of dross;
Within be fed, without be rich no more:
   So shalt thou feed on Death, that feeds on men,
    And Death once dead, there's no more dying then.

147

My love is as a fever, longing still
For that which longer nurseth the disease;
Feeding on that which doth preserve the ill,
Th' uncertain sickly appetite to please.
My reason, the physician to my love,
Angry that his prescriptions are not kept,
Hath left me, and I desperate now approve
Desire is death, which physic did except.
Past cure I am, now reason is past care,
And frantic-mad with evermore unrest;
My thoughts and my discourse as madmen's are,
At random from the truth vainly expressed;
   For I have sworn thee fair, and thought thee bright,
    Who art as black as hell, as dark as night.

148

O me, what eyes hath Love put in my head,
Which have no correspondence with true sight!
Or, if they have, where is my judgement fled,
That censures falsely what they see aright?
If that be fair whereon my false eyes dote,
What means the world to say it is not so?
If it be not, then love doth well denote
Love's eye is not so true as all men's: no.
How can it? O, how can Love's eye be true,
That is so vexed with watching and with tears?
No marvel, then, though I mistake my view;
The sun itself sees not till heaven clears.
    O cunning Love! with tears thou keep'st me blind,
    Lest eyes well-seeing thy foul faults should find.

149

Canst thou, O cruel! say I love thee not
When I, against myself, with thee partake?
Do I not think on thee, when I forgot
Am of myself, all tyrant for thy sake?
Who hateth thee that I do call my friend?
On whom frown'st thou that I do fawn upon?
Nay, if thou lour'st on me, do I not spend
Revenge upon myself with present moan?
What merit do I in myself respect,
That is so proud thy service to despise,
When all my best doth worship thy defect,
Commanded by the motion of thine eyes?
    But, love, hate on, for now I know thy mind;
    Those that can see thou lovest, and I am blind.

150

O, from what power hast thou this powerful might
With insufficiency my heart to sway?
To make me give the lie to my true sight,
And swear that brightness doth not grace the day?
Whence hast thou this becoming of things ill,
That in the very refuse of thy deeds
There is such strength and warrantise of skill,
That, in my mind, thy worst all best exceeds?
Who taught thee how to make me love thee more,
The more I hear and see just cause of hate?
O, though I love what others do abhor,
With others thou shouldst not abhor my state:
    If thy unworthiness raised love in me,
    More worthy I to be beloved of thee.

151

Love is too young to know what conscience is;
Yet who knows not conscience is born of love?
Then, gentle cheater, urge not my amiss,
Lest guilty of my faults thy sweet self prove:
For, thou betraying me, I do betray
My nobler part to my gross body's treason;
My soul doth tell my body that he may
Triumph in love; flesh stays no farther reason;
But, rising at thy name, doth point out thee
As his triumphant prize. Proud of this pride,
He is contented thy poor drudge to be,
To stand in thy affairs, fall by thy side,
    No want of conscience hold it that I call
    Her 'love' for whose dear love I rise and fall.

152

In loving thee thou know'st I am forsworn,
But thou art twice forsworn, to me love swearing;
In act thy bed-vow broke, and new faith torn
In vowing new hate after new love bearing.
But why of two oaths' breach do I accuse thee,
When I break twenty? I am perjured most;
For all my vows are oaths but to misuse thee,
And all my honest faith in thee is lost.
For I have sworn deep oaths of thy deep kindness,
Oaths of thy love, thy truth, thy constancy;
And, to enlighten thee, gave eyes to blindness,
Or made them swear against the thing they see;
 For I have sworn thee fair; more perjured eye,
 To swear against the truth so foul a lie!

153

Cupid laid by his brand, and fell asleep:
A maid of Dian's this advantage found,
And his love-kindling fire did quickly steep
In a cold valley-fountain of that ground;
Which borrow'd from this holy fire of Love
A dateless lively heat, still to endure,
And grew a seething bath which yet men prove
Against strange maladies a sovereign cure.
But at my mistress' eye Love's brand new-fired,
The boy for trial needs would touch my breast;
I, sick withal, the help of bath desired,
And thither hied, a sad distemper'd guest,
 But found no cure: the bath for my help lies
 Where Cupid got new fire – my mistress' eyes.

154

The little Love-god lying once asleep
Laid by his side his heart-inflaming brand,
Whilst many nymphs that vow'd chaste life to keep
Came tripping by; but in her maiden hand
The fairest votary took up that fire,
Which many legions of true hearts had warm'd;
And so the general of hot desire
Was sleeping by a virgin hand disarm'd.
This brand she quenched in a cool well by,
Which from Love's fire took heat perpetual,
Growing a bath and healthful remedy
For men diseased; but I, my mistress' thrall,
 Came there for cure, and this by that I prove,
 Love's fire heats water, water cools not love.

INDEX OF FIRST LINES

Selected Further Reading

The Complete Works of William Shakespeare
Nothing Like the Sun by Anthony Burgess (London, 1964)
Shakespeare by Anthony Burgess (London, 1970)
Shakespeare's Sonnets edited by Stephen Booth (London, 1977)
Shakespeare: A Life by Park Honan (Oxford, 1998)